THE LIBRARY OF AMERICAN ART

SAMUEL F. B. MORSE

Samuel F. B. Morse

WILLIAM KLOSS

Harry N. Abrams, Inc., Publishers, New York
IN ASSOCIATION WITH
The National Museum of American Art, Smithsonian Institution

For Charles Timbrell

Series Director: Margaret L. Kaplan
Editor: Janet Wilson
Series Designer: Michael Hentges
Photo Research: Neil Hoos

Library of Congress Cataloging-in-Publication Data

Kloss, William.
  Samuel F. B. Morse / William Kloss.
    p. cm.
  Includes index.
  Bibliography: p. 155
  ISBN 0-8109-1531-6
  1. Morse, Samuel Finley Breese, 1791–1872—Criticism and
interpretation.   2. Portrait painting, American.   3. Portrait
painting—19th century—United States.   4. Narrative painting,
American.   I. Title.
  ND237.M75K56 1988
  759.13—dc19   88–5879

NOTE ON THE DATES: The dates given for the paintings may differ
from previously published dates. Using recent scholarship, stylistic
analysis, and a careful reading of the documents, the author has
tried to date the works as closely as possible.

Frontispiece:

Self-Portrait. c. 1818. Oil on wood, 10½×8½"
Collection of the Brick Store Museum, Kennebunk, Maine

*This handsome painting has been little noticed. Once on loan to the Addison
Gallery at Phillips Academy, property of an Andover resident, it was given by
her to the Brick Store Museum in 1948. Although it bears no inscription and
seems to be unmentioned in the correspondence or other literature, it has tradi-
tionally been called a self-portrait. There is no reason to doubt it.*

Text copyright © 1988 William Kloss

Illustrations copyright © 1988 Harry N. Abrams, Inc.
Published in 1988 by Harry N. Abrams, Incorporated, New York
A Times Mirror Company

Printed and bound in Japan

Contents

Preface

D O YOU SUPPOSE IT'S THE SAME MORSE?" This question is often heard in museums when looking at paintings by Samuel F. B. Morse. Those who do not know that he painted are surprised to find, and sometimes oddly reluctant to believe, that the inventor of the telegraph was also an artist. A different response is surprisingly common among those more familiar with American art: "Of course, he didn't paint very much." This reflects their knowledge that Morse, frustrated in his attempts to paint significant historical subjects, ceased to paint midway through his adult life. Accompanying these misconceptions is the mistaken conclusion that he cannot have been a very good painter.

This book is an attempt to change those perceptions by presenting to a wider public a substantial number of Morse's paintings, examining them critically and tracing the artistic and intellectual life of this intriguing man who not only changed history with his invention but also recorded history in his painting. That it was a record of American people rather than American events was a disappointment for Morse. It should not be for us. We can recognize, as James Thomas Flexner did thirty years ago, that Morse practiced portraiture "without affectation, [and] gave full sway to that creative realism" that was the special mark of his genius.

This is a study of art in a biographical context. It is not a complete life of Morse. Carleton Mabee's biography (1943) is not likely to be surpassed soon for an exhaustive probing of the multifaceted Morse. My book could hardly have been written without Mabee's; nonetheless, Morse the artist plays a smaller role in his book than it did in Morse's own mind.

Anyone familiar with recent art-historical scholarship on Morse's paintings knows that Paul J. Staiti has supplied the essential framework for their study. In his continuing publications, Staiti has unearthed "lost" paintings, examined questions of patronage, and discussed the ideological and intellectual basis of Morse's art. My debt to him is obvious, and I gratefully acknowledge it.

These and other sources may be found in the bibliography. Throughout the text and the captions are numerous quotations by or about Morse's sitters. Some of these will be found in the readily available published literature, but many others have been culled from genealogies, memoirs, diaries, and other less accessible records.

I am deeply beholden to Margaret L. Kaplan of Harry N. Abrams, who gave me the opportunity to write the book and showed forbearance during the process. Though not listed here, the many, many persons who have graciously furthered my efforts with their own—collectors, curators, librarians, and historians—have my abiding gratitude. Among them, I want to express particular thanks, together with unqualified admiration for her professional skills and spirit of cooperation, to Donna Belle Garvin of the New Hampshire Historical Society in Concord.

Richard M. Candee, architectural historian, director of the Preservation Studies Program at Boston University, and valued friend, guided me through the intricate byways of New England past and present, leading to discoveries and rediscoveries and demonstrating the virtue of persistence.

Marc Pachter, historian at the National Portrait Gallery, in his customary concise and penetrating manner, counseled me on the biographer's art. Where I have approached the mark, I am immeasurably obligated to him.

WILLIAM KLOSS
Washington, D.C.

Introduction

Engraving after a painting by
Alonzo Chappel
Samuel F. B. Morse

Published in 1872. National Portrait Gallery,
Smithsonian Institution, Washington, D.C.

*To his son Willie he wrote, "I have been
very busy lately attending upon the great
men here with whom I have business of importance . . . and on Wednesday the 16th
instant, your uncle & I were presented at
Court to the Emperor & Empress. It
would have dazzled your young eyes to see
the show of diamonds and pearls, and glit-
tering decorations . . . and I don't think
you would have known your father."*

"YOUR NAME, SIR, IS WELL KNOWN HERE." Thus Napoleon III greeted Samuel F. B. Morse on January 16, 1867, when the elderly American visitor was presented at the French court. It was a moment of no little irony. Morse, who had once run for mayor of the City of New York on the Native American ticket, had long been anti-alien and anti-Catholic. Although disaffected from current politics at home, he remained a firm patriot. But for the aristocratic occasion this pious son of a Calvinist pastor had ordered up a full suit of court clothes replete with gold lace, cashmere vest, small sword, and, "for *extra*ordinary mortals, like my humble republican self, . . . all my orders, seven decorations, covering my left breast."

The irony of the occasion was not entirely lost on Morse. Though by then world renowned as the developer of the electric telegraph, he had endured many setbacks in his professional pursuits, and it is obvious that the attentions of the emperor soothed old wounds. Later that summer he reported an incident ("for family use only") during the procession of the European heads of state at the Hôtel de Ville: "Sarah and I were standing upon two chairs overlooking the front rank of [spectators]. The emperor gave an unusual and special bow to me, which I returned, and he then, with a smile, gave me a second bow so marked as to draw the attention of those around, who at once turned to see to whom this courtesy was shown."

Had his life unfolded as he had once intended, Morse would have wished the emperor to recognize him as an artist, a vocation he had pursued for some thirty years and forsaken for as many by 1867. Among his varied professions none had meant as much to him as that of painter, one moreover who had hoped to emulate the tradition exemplified by the vast collection in the Louvre. That museum's treasures had, in fact, served as the subject for one of his finest paintings years before.

When the art section of the Universal Exposition opened in June, 1867, its conservative character sparked considerable controversy and publicity. In contrast to this work were the iconoclastic paintings of Edouard Manet and Gustave Courbet, who staged their own exhibitions in independent pavilions. Yet there is no evidence that Morse ever visited the art exhibitions or showed any interest in either the conservative or the progressive art of the period. Instead, as honorary commissioner of the United States to the Paris exposition (appointed in early May, 1867), he wrote a detailed report on the electrical section.

8

Morse's profession as an inventor and entrepreneur dominated the second half of his adult life. Actually his fascination with mechanical technology and electrical science had begun much earlier, and was as deep-seated as his attraction to art. Morse must be ranked high among Americans of the revolutionary and federal eras whose lives were distinguished by the breadth of their interests and knowledge and their success in varied endeavors. Those of the older generations—including Benjamin Franklin, Thomas Jefferson, Francis Hopkinson, Charles Willson Peale, and Benjamin Rush—were guided by the political conviction of the American Enlightenment that, in Jefferson's words, "if a nation expects to be ignorant and free . . . it expects what never was and never will be."

From our distance the men of Morse's generation—the generation born during the first decade of government under the Constitution—seem to have been guided by more pragmatic, less idealistic desires. Yet in fact they started from the reiterated Jeffersonian principle that significant knowledge was *useful* knowledge that would promote the prosperity of the community, and from that premise they embarked upon an extraordinary three-quarters of a century of technological invention and territorial expansion that utterly transformed the country—and the world—within Morse's lifetime.

Engraving after a painting by Alonzo Chappel
Napoleon III

Published in 1870. National Portrait Gallery, Smithsonian Institution, Washington, D.C.

"The great ideal, the inspiration of his life, [was] pleasing everyone, and himself at the same time." (William Bolitho)

From 1793, when Eli Whitney introduced the cotton gin, to 1866, when Cyrus Field laid the first permanently successful Atlantic cable, the roll call of American inventions—from the iron and steel plows to the reaper, from the steamboat to the electric train, from the typesetting machine to the Colt revolver, from the power loom to the sewing machine—continues to astonish us. And the centerpiece of this burgeoning inventiveness was Morse's telegraph. Precisely because it provided instantaneous communication between the most distant places, the telegraph had a more immediate and profound impact upon society than any of the other inventions mentioned. While they might revolutionize productivity and distribution, the telegraph enabled man to know what was happening as it was happening, anywhere that the wires could reach. It was the first enormous step in the shrinking of the world to the interdependent global community of today.

It was as an entrepreneur that Morse approached the problems and potential of the electric telegraph and of the communication code that bears his name. Much of his energy following his invention was devoted to securing patents in the United States and abroad. He was repeatedly frustrated in his efforts to secure foreign patents. Indeed, during the 1867 exposition in Paris Morse encountered an Englishman at the telegraph display who asked why he had nothing on exhibition. With some bitterness, Morse replied, "Nothing? Why I can scarcely pass by the telegraph instruments whether in the Exposition, or in all the Offices of the Continent, and in England too, that I do not hear the cry of *father* from almost every one of them."

As an entrepreneur, he associated himself with Cyrus Field in the 1850s and 1860s in the attempt to lay the Atlantic cable, whose inevitability Morse had first predicted. In a somewhat different spirit more in tune with his artis-

CHRISTIAN SCHUSSELE (1826–1879)
Men of Progress

1862. Oil on canvas, 51⅜ x 76¾"
National Portrait Gallery, Smithsonian Institution,
Washington, D.C.

In this pantheon of inventors, Morse occupies the place of honor, his telegraphic instrument at his hand, in tribute to the primacy of that invention in the first sixty years of the century. Among the other men are Samuel Colt and Cyrus McCormick, third and fourth from the left, and Elias Howe and Erastus Bigelow, first and fourth from the right. All are accompanied by models or drawings of their inventions, and Benjamin Franklin, father of them all, is present in the portrait on the wall.

tic interests, he was the first to describe the daguerreotype process to Americans, and among its first American practitioners. He and Louis Daguerre, its French inventor, became friends, and Morse used his influence to get Daguerre elected to an honorary membership in the National Academy of Design, of which Morse was president. Both men were painters, and both seem to have been primarily interested in the new process as an aid to painting through the revelation of detail.

Because Morse's politics had a significant impact on his life as a painter, and because they darkened the public perception of him on more than one occasion, their origins are of interest to us. Morse was born into a family that was, we may say, politically engaged in the theological arena. The vitriolic, albeit principled, battles between the orthodox Puritan Calvinists (among whom his father, the Reverend Jedidiah Morse, was a stalwart) and the liberal Unitarians divided many congregational and intellectual communities, necessarily affecting the body politic as well. Jedidiah Morse helped found Andover Theological Seminary to protect the faith, and he sent Finley (as Samuel was called in the family) to his own alma mater, Yale, which was free from the dangers of Harvard's new Unitarian heterodoxy.

Because of the close ties with English Congregationalism, many people of the Calvinist persuasion were to be numbered as Tories before and Federalists after the Revolution. They were inclined to sympathize with England during the War of 1812. Among them were Morse's parents, but Samuel, by then in England and smarting from English verbal barbs, took the opposite stand. Later, however, he became as conservative as they had been.

The entangling of religion and politics that displeased Jefferson was a significant fact of American society throughout much of the nineteenth century. Morse's sincere piety motivated his campaigns for public office, his pamphleteering, even his pro-slavery stance. It is also evident in the famous phrase (though selected by another) that inaugurated the first telegraph line: "What hath God wrought!"

Morse returned to New York from Paris in May, 1868. At the end of December he was honored as the "father of Modern Telegraphy" at a banquet at Delmonico's, then on Fifth Avenue at Fourteenth Street. His former pupil Daniel Huntington reminded the guests that "every studio is more or less a laboratory. The painter is a chemist delving into . . . occult arts by which the inward light is made to gleam from the canvas, and the warm flesh to glow and palpitate. The studio of my beloved master . . . was indeed a laboratory. Vigorous, life-like portraits, poetic and historic groups . . . grew upon his easel; but there were many hours . . . when absorbed in study among galvanic batteries and mysterious lines of wires, he seemed to us like an alchemist of the middle ages in search of the philosopher's stone." He added, "We grieved to see the sketch upon the canvas untouched."

But Samuel F. B. Morse, a man of many parts, had painted hundreds of "vigorous, life-like portraits" before he turned his attention definitively to other pursuits. As they become better known again, they may demonstrate that the "father of Modern Telegraphy" was also the finest portrait painter of his generation.

Morse's First Telegraphic
Reception Device

c. 1833–38. National Museum of American
History, Smithsonian Institution,
Washington, D.C.

It was this instrument that was demonstrated before President Van Buren, February 21, 1838, resulting in a congressional appropriation of $30,000 to install a Washington-to-Baltimore telegraph line. The rectangular frame is puzzling until it is recognized as a canvas stretcher! It was at hand when Morse needed it.

I. "I Was Made for a Painter"

An East Haven, Connecticut, painter and sculptor in wax, Moulthrop attained unusual dignity and intensity in this large painting.

Reverend Jedidiah Morse

Painted in the stiff linear manner of the self-taught artist, this portrait of the Reverend Morse (1761–1826) is remarkably bold in color, with a bright red collar accenting the gold and bronze robe. The hypnotic eyes of the schematic but forceful head are tellingly aligned with the titles of Jedidiah's geographies, while a volume of his sermons rests on the shelf above them.

SAMUEL MORSE WAS NOT YET TEN when his father wrote to him at Phillips Academy (February 21, 1801): "Your natural disposition, my dear son, renders it proper for me earnestly to recommend to you to *attend to one thing at a time*. It is impossible that you can do two things well at the same time, and I would, therefore, never have you attempt it." Although his parents regularly issued such admonitions, their son came by his temperament honestly, as they might have recognized.

His father, Jedidiah Morse, was more than a New England Calvinist pastor; he was America's first geographer, whose publications included *Geography Made Easy* (1784), *The American Geography* (1789), and *The American Gazetteer* (1797). The first of these, written while he was employed as a schoolteacher in New Haven, enjoyed twenty-five editions during the author's lifetime, and the second had multiple editions in Europe as well as America. Indeed, the latter was intended not only for Americans but also for Europeans, who, wrote Morse, "have been the sole writers of American Geography, and have too often suffered fancy to supply the place of facts." The facts compiled in Morse's geographies were demographic, economic, and political as well as physical and biological. The reader might learn, for example, that 683,070 bricks and 2,438 bags of cotton were exported from the United States between October 1, 1792, and September 30, 1793.

Nor were these the only literary endeavors of the Reverend Mr. Morse. He wrote pamphlets defending orthodox Calvinism and attacking the Unitarians so vigorously that it has been said he did more than any other person to drive them from the Congregational community. He wrote the article on America for the first American edition of the Encyclopaedia Britannica (1790). He coauthored *A Compendious History of New England* (1804) and at the end of his life published his *Annals of the American Revolution* (1824).

Jedidiah Morse's celebrity assured that his portrait had been taken a number of times by the turn of the century. When, probably at the age of nineteen, Samuel Morse painted a portrait of his father, it was as a scholar in his study rather than a preacher in his pulpit. With his geography books and a globe behind him, pen in hand, rapt in thoughtful dignity, *Reverend Jedidiah Morse* is an American descendant of the noble line of scholar portraits going back to Albrecht Dürer and beyond. America's clerics were often her scholars as well, and when Morse painted this example, there was already a rich tradition of portraits of such men, especially among Connecticut painters. Winthrop Chandler and

Reverend Jedidiah Morse

John Bartlett

1809. Watercolor on paper, 4⅜ x 3″
Yale University Art Gallery,
New Haven, Connecticut
Gift of Mrs. Hilles Peterson

Bartlett (1784–1866) received his B.A. from Yale in 1807, but remained at the college for two years studying theology under Yale President Timothy Dwight, who was a close friend of the Reverend Morse. Licensed to preach in 1810, Bartlett spent most of his life in Connecticut, much plagued by "bodily infirmity," although living to be eighty-one.

Ralph Earl had worked in the genre, and the New Haven artist Reuben Moulthrop (Jedidiah's contemporary) painted *Reverend Ammi Ruhamah Robbins*, which, though full length and slightly later than Morse's depiction of his father, is representative of this type of portrait and quite similar in many details.

This was not Morse's first painting. After boarding school at Phillips Academy, Andover, he had entered Yale College in October, 1805. Though he may have been taught the principles of drawing together with penmanship at home in Charlestown, Massachusetts, and at Andover, it was at Yale that he began to draw and paint with some diligence. Starting off with caricatures, he then moved on to serious likenesses of classmates and faculty, and soon experienced the pleasure of being paid for his skill. "I employ all my leisure time in painting," he wrote to his parents in August, 1809. "I have a great number of persons engaged to be drawn on ivory, no less than seven. They obtain the ivories for themselves." Within ten months he was able to report: "My price is five dollars for a miniature on ivory... [and] my price for profiles is one dollar, and everybody is ready to engage me at that price."

One classmate who availed himself of the bargain profile portrait was John Bartlett (soon to be the Reverend Bartlett), whose likeness of 1809 is probably Morse's earliest signed and dated work. The incipient Romanticism in the tousled hair, emphatic eyebrows, and rather high color suggests that Morse had already made the acquaintance of Washington Allston's poetic portraits, and perhaps of Allston himself. The expressive miniature portraits of Edward Malbone, Allston's close friend, may also have been known to Morse.

It seems probable that Morse first met Allston when the latter visited his mother in New Haven just after his marriage in June, 1809. In July, 1810, just graduated from Yale, Morse asked his father to arrange for him to study with Allston: "As to my choice of a profession, I still think that I was made for a painter.... I should desire to study with [Allston] during the winter, and, as he expects to return to England in the spring, I should admire to be able to go with him."

A second watercolor profile, possibly even earlier although undated, is of an older Yale student, Gideon Tomlinson. Tomlinson (B.A., 1802) received his M.A. from the college in 1808—one reason for supposing the likeness dates from that year. Just as significant, there is no hint of the expressive edge seen in the Bartlett portrait. While both watercolors are pure profiles, the Tomlinson is more linear, more classically restrained, with less suggestion of volume in the figure. It has antecedents in the popular profile portraits of the European artists Charles Saint-Mémin and James Sharples, active in the United States from about 1793 until about 1810.

Despite his extracurricular activity, Morse did not neglect his classes. But he was less interested in Homer than in Jeremiah Day's lectures on electricity and Benjamin Silliman's chemistry course in which batteries were studied. Day and Silliman belong to both of Morse's careers. They started him on the road to the invention of the telegraph, and also had their portraits painted by him.

I WAS MADE FOR A PAINTER

At Yale Morse decided that he would be a painter. His pride in his chosen profession is manifest in the charming watercolor *Self-Portrait*, painted about 1809–10. It is our only example of his portraits on ivory, the five-dollar variety. The more complicated three-quarter pose must have been used for all the ivories, and the greater technical demand was surely worth the additional four dollars. Although the foreshortening of the arms gives him trouble, he catches his candid expression with delicacy and easy confidence. It is the appealing optimism of one embarking on his career.

It should be emphasized that Morse shows himself with the palette and brush of a painter in oils, not watercolors, though that is his medium here. We may assume that he was already painting in oils and that this miniature dates somewhat later than is usually presumed. It could be contemporary with the portrait of his father already discussed, perhaps as late as the fall of 1810, when he was once again at home in Charlestown. That it appears more suave than the portrait of Jedidiah is explained by the small ivory, so much easier to command than the large panel. The influence of Allston and Edward Malbone is especially apparent here; several of their miniatures show markedly similar heads.

The rest of Morse's immediate family consisted of his mother and his two younger brothers. Elizabeth Ann Breese Morse, whose maternal grandfather, Samuel Finley, had been president of Princeton (then called the College of New Jersey), and whose father, Samuel Breese, was the prosperous founder of Shrewsbury on the New Jersey coast, conferred the names of both gentlemen on her firstborn son (1791), Samuel Finley Breese Morse.

She also endowed her son with a spirited, forthright nature and a robust constitution. Of ten other children born to the Morses, only two boys survived infancy: Sidney Edwards (born 1794) and Richard Cary (1795). It is always startling to be reminded of the infant mortality rate of an earlier age. When he was thirteen, Samuel wrote to his brothers at Andover: "I now write you again to inform you that Mama had a baby, but it was born dead & has just been buried, now you have three brothers & three sisters in heaven and I hope you & I will meet them there at our death."

Samuel Morse depicted the whole family together in a gouache that was ambitious in its attempt at grouping full-length figures in an interior, but nonetheless seems stylistically closer to the first miniature portraits than to the *Self-Portrait*. In the *Morse Family Portrait* both the remarkably plump Mrs. Morse and her youngest son, Richard, are depicted in strict profile, as were the Tomlinson and Bartlett watercolors. Samuel (left) and Sidney each stand in a three-quarter pose, while their father is presented frontally. The hierarchical effect of this symmetry is modified by linking Samuel with his mother and Sidney with his father.

These pairings do not seem coincidental or insignificant. Samuel not only bore the Breese and Finley names but had much of his mother's practical and independent turn of mind. Here he even seems to share some of her bulk! Sidney, whose slender elegance echoes Jedidiah's, would in a few years publish a

Gideon Tomlinson

c. 1808. Watercolor on paper, oval, 4¼ x 3¼"
Yale University Art Gallery,
New Haven, Connecticut
Gift of the Associates in Fine Arts

Tomlinson (1780–1854) had a distinguished career as a lawyer in New Haven and Fairfield. A Democrat, he served in the House of Representatives (1819–27), as governor of Connecticut (1827–31) and, as an anti-Jackson Whig, in the U.S. Senate (1831–37). His portrait also appears in Morse's 1822 House of Representatives, in profile, standing by the fifth column from the right.

defense of his father against a charge of plagiarism and later collaborate with him on revising the famous *Geography* and editing another. Moreover, he founded two influential religious newspapers. The boys' characters and affinities were already clearly established when this family gathering was painted, and Samuel has duly noted them.

As in the single portrait of him, the Reverend Morse is shown as a scholar. With the globe before him as the focus of all eyes, he discourses to his family on geography. Richard's hand touches a geography book with a foldout map. Mrs. Morse has put aside her sewing. The seriousness of the gathering is seconded by the refinement of the setting. Placed against an elaborately paneled fireplace and mantel, with flanking arches, the family is grouped around an elegant American Chippendale table flanked by two Chippendale side chairs. The floor is covered with a carpet that features floral patterns in large panels of alternating geometric designs. (This carpet—and the tilt of the floor—is comparable to that seen in the Moulthrop portrait of Reverend Ammi Ruhamah Robbins.) A note of domestic warmth is provided by the sewing basket with lid casually ajar, near which a black-and-orange cat reposes. Despite some awkwardnesses, this small painting is a surprisingly imposing piece.

In the winter and spring of 1810–11, Morse worked for a Boston bookseller, Daniel Mallory, who was also among Jedidiah's publishers. Although he chafed at the time lost from painting, he managed to attend lectures on anatomy given by Dr. Benjamin Waterhouse and Dr. John C. Warren, both of the Harvard Medical School, and to paint during the evenings. The anatomy lectures made use of European illustrated texts, and it must have been at this time that Morse made his drawing (actually pencil and oil) of the back view of *The Farnese Hercules*, which is on the verso of the contemporary portrait of his father.

This drawing is not from a cast, but of an *écorché*—a flayed figure—revealing the anatomical structure. It is, in fact, a literal transcription of an engraved plate in Bernardino Genga's *Anatomia per uso et intelligenza del Disegno* (Rome, 1691), a folio intended for the instruction of artists. To this end famous examples of ancient sculpture were rendered as anatomical models. The drawings accompanying Genga's text were done by Charles Errard, director of the French Academy in Rome. The book was translated into English (London, 1723), with the plates "Re-Engraved by the Ablest Hands in England," and this was probably the edition seen by Morse. His drawing, like the print, shows the famous statue in reverse. This represents Morse's first known contact, however slight, with ancient sculpture.

More important was his increased contact with Washington Allston, whose informal student he had become. Undoubtedly it was Allston who guided Morse in the conception of his first history painting, *The Landing of the Pilgrims at Plymouth*, painted during the first five months of 1811. To the eyes of many Charlestown residents—the painting hung for many years over the entrance door in the old Town Hall—it must have been impressive if only in its strangeness. For the first time Morse had attempted a large, multifigure oil

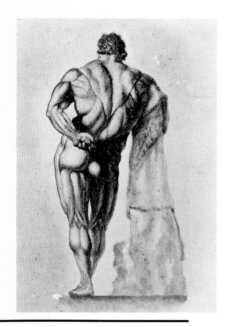

The Farnese Hercules
verso of portrait of Reverend Jedidiah Morse

1810–11. Pencil and oil on wood, 12½ x 5½"
Yale University Art Gallery,
New Haven, Connecticut

One of the most famous statues of antiquity, it served as a model for painters from the time of its rediscovery in the middle of the sixteenth century.

Morse Family Portrait

c. 1809–10. Watercolor, gouache,
pen and ink on paper, 19¼ x 24¼"
National Museum of American History,
Smithsonian Institution, Washington, D.C.

"Dear Brother,—I am sitting in the parlor in the armchair on the right of the fireplace.... As I turn my eyes upward and opposite I behold the family picture painted by an ingenious artist who, I understand, is at present residing in London. If you are acquainted with him, give my love to him and my best wishes for his prosperity and success in the art to which, if report says true, he has devoted himself with much diligence" (Sidney to Samuel, January 18, 1812).

I WAS MADE FOR A PAINTER

Morse Family Portrait

Self-Portrait

c. 1809–10. Watercolor on ivory, 3¼ x 2⅝"
National Academy of Design, New York

The subtlety of modeling and color is especially striking in the careful blend of white and ivory tones in the shirt and collar.

painting and, most significantly, one that depicted figures in movement. He had probably never seen such a work. Allston's figure paintings—those at hand in Boston—were small, and in any event his historical figures were more apt to be engaged in oratorical than dramatic interaction. But Allston had already had direct experience of Renaissance art, and in this case it may be inferred that he shared his knowledge of Raphael (possibly through the intermediary of Marcantonio Raimondi's engravings) with his young protégé. Certainly the self-consciously elaborate poses (especially the mirror reversal of the central figures) of Morse's *Pilgrims* suggest the study of Raphaelesque compositions.

It is easy but unfair to criticize severely this first attempt at an unknown genre. Just as John Singleton Copley had been unable to compose a coherent

The Landing of the Pilgrims at Plymouth

1811. Oil on canvas, 45 x 60"
Courtesy of the Trustees of
the Boston Public Library

Earlier examples of the subject invariably show very small figures in a coastal landscape setting. Although some of the paintings are comparable in size to the Morse, and certain motifs may seem superficially similar, Morse's conception of this subject as a history painting dominated by heroic figures is entirely new.

group of figures before seeing European art, so Morse could not, despite Allston's guidance. It is said that Allston, and Gilbert Stuart as well, put the stamp of approval on *The Landing of the Pilgrims*, thus persuading Jedidiah Morse to make the considerable sacrifice necessary to finance his son's study abroad. Their praise of this student production was a white lie in the cause of an American aspirant to the art of painting.

They chose their candidate well. Samuel Morse set sail for England with the Allstons on July 13, 1811; arrived at Liverpool on August 7; reached London on the 15th; and by September 3 could report that Benjamin West, the American-born artist now renowned as president of the Royal Academy, had told him that one of his drawings "was an extraordinary production, that I had talent, and only wanted knowledge of the art to make a great painter."

What astonished Morse above all was "to find such a difference in the encouragement of art between this country and America. In America it seemed to lie neglected, and only thought to be an employment suited to a lower class of people; but here it is the constant subject of conversation, and . . . no person is esteemed accomplished or well educated unless he possesses almost an enthusiastic love for paintings." It was this discovery that was to fire Samuel F. B. Morse for the next twenty-five years in his determination to raise the practice and appreciation of art in America to the level he had experienced in England.

II. *"The Intellectual Branch of the Art"*

WILLIAM HOGARTH
The Enraged Musician

November, 1741. Etching and
engraving, 13⅛ x 15¾"
National Gallery of Art, Washington, D.C.

"I don't know how many times I have run to the window expecting to see some poor creature in the agonies of death" (Morse letter, September 17, 1811).

Benjamin West

c. 1824–26. Oil on canvas, 30 x 25"
National Academy of Design, New York

Charles Robert Leslie copied the 1811 portrait of West (1738–1820) by Sir Thomas Lawrence at West's request. The surface handling of Morse's copy suggests a date in the 1820s. It seems likely that Morse made his copy after Leslie's, which was shown at the Boston Atheneum in 1824.

ALMOST FROM THE MOMENT OF HIS ARRIVAL in England in 1811, Morse found himself of two minds about his hosts and their habits. There was the fear of being cheated that seems universal among first-time travelers in a foreign country: "I found myself in a land of strangers, liable to be cheated out of my teeth almost" (August 15). And the odd customs: "A person to be genteel must rise at twelve o'clock, breakfast at two, dine at six, and sup at the same time, and go to bed about three o'clock the next morning" (August 17). "The cries of London, of which you have doubtless heard, are very annoying to me.... they all appear to be the cries of distress. Hogarth's picture of the enraged musician will give you an excellent idea of the noise I hear every day under my windows" (September 17).

On the other hand, there was the partiality toward culture that Morse longed for: "I was surprised on entering the gallery of paintings in the British Institution, at seeing eight or ten *ladies*...employed in copying some of the pictures. You can see from this circumstance in what estimation the art is held here, since ladies of distinction, without hesitation or reserve, are willing to draw in public" (August 24).

Most of all, however, his introduction to the Old World was complicated by the rapidly deteriorating relations between America and England. "The accounts lately received from America look rather gloomy" (September 17). "In case of war I shall be ordered out of the country. If so, instead of returning home, had I not better go to Paris, as...there are great advantages there? I only ask the question in case of war" (September 24). When the United States declared war on England the following June, 1812, the personal consequences for Morse were considerable. Although there was never any real threat of his being expelled from England, he rapidly developed anti-Federalist views that were anathema to his staunchly Federalist parents. He began to speak up in English company whenever he heard America denigrated. It is likely that these years spent in a country at war with his own fueled his republicanism and his nascent xenophobia.

Despite political distractions, Morse pursued his art fervently. "My passion for my art," he wrote his parents on September 20, 1812, "is so firmly rooted that I am confident no human power could destroy it,...and I never shall be able sufficiently to show my gratitude to my parents for their indulgence in so enabling me to pursue that profession without which I am sure I

Benjamin West

would be miserable." Almost a year before, probably in October, 1811, his chalk drawing from a small cast of the *Laocoön* had gained him admission to the evening classes of the Royal Academy, where drawing from casts and from ancient originals in the British Museum was the basic method of instruction.

An even earlier drawing of an ancient sculpture, however, was apparently made from a small cast of *The Farnese Hercules*, already familiar to him from the anatomical version he had copied in Boston. As related in 1834 by the painter William Dunlap, who was also the first historian of American art, Morse, after working for two weeks on this drawing, showed it to West, who responded, "Very well, sir, very well, go on and finish it."

"It *is* finished."

"Oh, no, look here, and here, and here."

After a week of reworking: "Very well, indeed, sir, go on and finish it."

"Is it not finished?"

"Not yet. See, you have not marked that muscle, nor the articulations of the finger joints."

After several more days: "Very clever, indeed. Well, sir, go on and finish it."

"I cannot finish it."

West relented: "Well, I have tried you long enough; now, sir, you have learned more by this drawing than you would have accomplished in double the time by a dozen half-finished drawings. It is not numerous drawings, but the *character of one*, which makes a thorough draughtsman. *Finish* one picture, sir, and you are a painter."

Even before *The Farnese Hercules*, Morse had drawn from "the head of Demosthenes...to get accustomed to handling black and white chalk. I shall then commence a drawing for the purpose of trying to enter the Royal Academy" (August 24, 1811). The latter was perhaps the *Hercules*, which cost him such pains, but although "Mr. Allston told me it would undoubtedly admit me...[he] advised me to draw another and remedy some defects in handling the chalks" (September 3).

The new candidate was to be *The Gladiator*, probably designating *The Borghese Gladiator*. A bronze cast of this work, particularly praised for its anatomical accuracy, had been one of the most famous sculptures in England since the time of Charles I. "After I had finished it I was displeased with it, and concluded not to offer it, but to attempt another. I have accordingly drawn another from the Laocoön statue, the most difficult of all the statues; have shown it to the keeper of the Academy and *am admitted for a year* without the least difficulty."

Morse painted during the day, and by November, 1811, he had copied West's copy of a Van Dyck portrait, finished one landscape, and begun another—"a morning scene at sunrise, which Mr. Allston is very much pleased with." By the end of January the four-month total was two landscapes and three portraits, including "one of myself...and [one] of Mr. Leslie, who is also taking mine." Charles Robert Leslie, only sixteen, had arrived from Philadelphia at the end of 1811, and he and Morse had taken rooms together at No. 82

Self-Portrait

c. 1812–13. Oil on canvas, 30 x 25″
Addison Gallery of American Art, Phillips
Academy, Andover, Massachusetts
Gift of Mrs. Leila Morse Rummel

To paint a profile self-portrait, a mirror is placed parallel to the left side of the artist's face, while a second mirror, into which he looks, is placed at a forty-five-degree angle on his right. In that mirror he will see the reflection of his left profile in the first mirror.

Self-Portrait

c. 1811–12. Oil on millboard, 10⅝ x 8⅞″
National Portrait Gallery, Smithsonian Institution,
Washington, D.C.
Gift of the James Smithson Society

It is rare for the forearms or hands to be indicated, even vaguely, in the bust-length portraits Morse had as models. It has been suggested that Allston's portrait of Francis Dana Channing (1808–09, private collection) is the primary influence. Morse's self-portrait, however, is more monumentally conceived, with the coat and cloak disposed in a massive pyramid rising from the bottom of the composition.

THE INTELLECTUAL BRANCH OF THE ART

Self-Portrait

CHARLES ROBERT LESLIE
Self-Portrait

1814. Oil on canvas, 29⅞ x 24¾"
National Portrait Gallery, London

Leslie (1794–1859) was never as committed to painting historical subjects as Morse, preferring realistic genre scenes from modern literature. He also painted official court scenes for Queen Victoria and published his Memoirs of the Life of John Constable *in 1843.*

Great Titchfield Street, where they painted in one room, "he at one window and I at the other," as Leslie recalled. Their portraits of each other, known to have been costume pieces—Leslie as a Spanish cavalier and Morse as a Scotsman in a tartan—are presently unlocated (Dunlap says they were kept as mementos by their landlady).

The *Self-Portrait* is, in all likelihood, the profile portrait now at the National Portrait Gallery in Washington. While profile portraits of other sitters are comparatively common, self-portraits in profile are rare. The reason may be the complexity of execution, since such a painting can be made only with the aid of two mirrors. The popularity of the pure profile can be attributed to the dogmas of Neoclassicism still current when Morse went to England.

The precise contours of ancient relief sculpture and, particularly, cameos and Greek vase painting made a profound impression on eighteenth-century artists and connoisseurs, from Johann Winckelmann to Joshua Reynolds ("a firm and determined outline is one of the characteristics of the great style in painting"). The vogue for the pure profile in late eighteenth-century figure painting is typified by a recherché subject that appears in paintings of the period: the story of the Corinthian maid who traces the outline of the shadow of her lover's head on the wall, thus inventing portraiture, indeed painting itself.

The reference to the antique suggests the possible significance of this small painting for Morse. The formal elegance and emotional disengagement that the pose embodies breathe the spirit of classicism. The pure profile was felt to be intellectually and even morally rigorous. Friedrich Schiller preferred pure outline to "those colors [that] do not tell me the truth." It is an endorsement of the principle of the ideal as stated by Reynolds: "It is this intellectual dignity . . . that ennobles the painter's art." And it manifests the desire of the aspiring artist to assume for himself the mantle of the "great style," and to excel, like West, "in the grandeur of his thought."

The supposition that the painting was a symbolic statement of artistic ambition is strengthened by the fact that Morse soon painted a lifesize version of the same composition. It is probably this painting of which he speaks in a letter to his parents of May 25, 1812: "I shall soon begin a portrait of myself and will try and send that to you." Now at Phillips Academy, this painting has the formal impact presaged by the smaller version. That impact is heightened by the brighter crimson swatch of drapery across the shoulder and torso (possibly the folded-back lining of the green cloak). Unfortunately the painting suffered severe loss during restoration some years ago. An overcleaning resulted in the removal of glazes, which did away with the subject's side whiskers and left him with a bad case of razor burn. The whiskers (seen in the small first version) were present until 1966; they are still evident in recent books illustrated with "pre-restoration" photographs.

This portrait may have been conceived in the spirit of harmonious competition and sharing of ideas that always characterized the deep friendship forged between Morse and Leslie. They had painted each other's portraits and now each painted a self-portrait in profile. Morse may have set the example, though the precocious Leslie's effort of 1814 may be thought the more advanced of the two, with its more persuasive volume and nearly trompe-l'oeil treatment of the hand.

This preoccupation with the antique, the classical, culminated in the inception of Morse's first truly large picture, *The Dying Hercules*, intended for the spring 1813 exhibition at the Royal Academy. He was inspired in this effort by the example of Allston's *The Dead Man Restored to Life by Touching the Bones of the Prophet Elisha*, a painting begun in 1811 and worked on for nearly three years. Its thirteen-by-ten-foot presence must have kindled a similar ambition in Allston's student. Morse's painting, a mere eight and a quarter by six and one-half feet, had only one figure compared with more than a dozen in *The Dead Man*. Its lesser complexity increased its scale and impact, while allowing Morse to complete and exhibit his *Hercules* a year before Allston finished his opus.

Allston's working method also influenced Morse. Allston made a small clay model to aid in the preparation of the head of his principal figure. It was a not uncommon practice among Renaissance artists, and Allston, whose love and knowledge of Venetian art was legend, would have been familiar with Vasari's accounts of this procedure by Tintoretto, among others. Morse did the same in 1812. "I have just finished a model in clay of a figure (the 'Dying Hercules'), my first attempt at sculpture. Mr. Allston is extremely pleased with it; he says it is better than all the things I have done since I have been in England put together, and says I must send a cast of it home to you, and that it will convince you that I shall make a painter. . . . I am now going to begin a picture of the death of Hercules from this figure, as large as life" (September 20).

Morse's increasingly passionate views on the political crisis in 1812 should be noted before taking a closer look at this painting. Ten days after America declared war on England, Mrs. Morse advised her son to "steer clear of any of the difficulties of the contest that is about to take place. We wish you to be very prudent and guarded in all your conversation and actions and not to make yourself a party man on either side." His father added a postscript: "Your mother has given you sound advice as respects the course you should pursue. Be the *artist* wholly and let *politics* alone."

In a vehement letter, Samuel replied: "I wish I could have a talk with you, papa; I am sure I could convince you that neither Federalists nor Democrats are Americans; that war with this country is just, and that the present Administration of our country has acted with perfect justice. . . . I could tell you volumes, but I have not time. . . . I only wish that among the infatuated party men I may not find my father, and I hope that he will be *neutral* rather than oppose the war measure. . . ." (August 6).

Samuel Morse did not let politics alone; instead they entered his art through allegorical allusion. Already, in his heated letter to his father, he had broken off his political harangue only to note pointedly that he was "painting a small historical piece; the subject is 'Marius in Prison,' and the soldier sent to kill him who

WASHINGTON ALLSTON
The Dead Man Restored to Life by Touching the Bones of the Prophet Elisha

1811–14. Oil on canvas, 156 x 120"
Pennsylvania Academy of the
Fine Arts, Philadelphia

The complex composition and poses are derived from a variety of Renaissance and ancient sources. In 1816 the Pennsylvania Academy agreed to buy the work for $3,500, the highest price ever paid to an American painter, and mortgaged the Academy building to meet part of the expense.

The Dying Hercules

1812. Plaster cast from clay original,
20 x 22½ x 9″
Yale University Art Gallery,
New Haven, Connecticut
Gift of the Reverend E. Goodrich Smith

"Mr. West also was extremely delighted with it. He said it was not merely an academical figure, but displayed mind and thought. He could not have made me a higher compliment." According to William Dunlap, West called in his son, Raphael, to see it and said, "Look there sir, I have always told you any painter can make a sculptor."

The Dying Hercules

1812–13. Oil on canvas, 96¼ x 78⅛″
Yale University Art Gallery,
New Haven, Connecticut
Gift of the artist

No buyer ever appeared for Morse's most ambitious history painting, and he eventually gave it to his alma mater.

drops his sword as Marius says, *'Durst thou kill Caius Marius?'* The historical fact you must be familiar with. I am taking great pains with it, and may possibly exhibit it in February at the British Gallery."

The abrupt and emphatic insertion of this information should give us pause. According to the account in Plutarch's *Lives*, the would-be executioner entered the dim room where the celebrated Roman, seven times consul, lay imprisoned and defenseless. "Marius's eyes, they say, seemed to the fellow to dart out flames at him, and a loud voice to say, out of the dark, 'Fellow, darest thou kill Caius Marius?' The barbarian . . . rushed out of doors, crying only this, 'I cannot kill Caius Marius.' " The story's simple and direct moral—that right makes might—had a contemporary relevance that could hardly have been lost on the Reverend Morse, even if he found it inapposite.

The *Marius in Prison*, if it was ever completed, has disappeared. But a similar case can be made for the political implications of the huge *Dying Hercules*. The subject is rarely encountered in art, bypassed for the accompanying incident of "Hercules hurling Lichas into the sea." Morse probably followed Ovid's version of the events leading to the death of Hercules (*Metamorphoses*, Book IX).

The Dying Hercules

When the duplicitous centaur Nessus offered to ferry Deianeira, Hercules' bride, across a raging river and then attempted to abduct her, Hercules felled him with an arrow. The dying Nessus, aware that Hercules had poisoned his arrows with the blood of the Lernaean Hydra he had slain as one of his famous "labors," persuaded Deianeira to take his bloodstained shirt because it would be a potent love potion if needed. Much later, with Hercules away from home, his wife heard rumors that he had transferred his affections to Iole, and so she sent the garment to Hercules "to strengthen anew her husband's dying love." Lichas delivered the garment to Hercules, who wrapped it around his shoulders, and the corrosive poison saturated his body. When he tried to remove it, "it dragged his skin with it and, horrible to tell, either clung to his limbs, resisting all attempts to pull it off, or left lacerated flesh, revealing his massive bones."

It is not a simple story, nor one in which we should seek too elaborate an allegory. But, in broader outlines, Morse must have seen America as the valiant hero who is treacherously deceived by a near relation. Hercules personifies courage and devotion to duty and has historically symbolized strong and virtuous government. Moreover, for his suffering, he was made immortal by Jupiter, and "when the . . . hero had put off his mortal shape . . . he began to appear greater than before, a majestic figure of august dignity."

A Hercules/America equation is also found in one of Morse's letters to his parents (July 10): "I have just heard of the unfortunate capture of the Chesapeake. Is our infant Hercules to be strangled at his birth? . . . I wish the British success against everything but *my country*." Public awareness of this allegorical allusion may be inferred from an engraving issued at the conclusion of the war, *Peace of Ghent 1814 and Triumph of America*, in which Hercules/America stands proud and dominant above a kneeling, submissive Britannia.

Morse's Hercules has considerable impact through size and bulk alone. He ignores the dynamism implicit in the story, stressing instead the hieratic pose, which becomes an ideogram of suffering virtue. While striving for the intellectual in art, Morse does not ignore the expressive potential of color and brushwork. The schematic, linear body is painted a high-toned pink and red—the artist's indication of the "consuming fire" of the poison that "hissed and boiled" in Hercules' blood "like white hot iron plunged into icy water." And the foreground, rocks, and sky receive a very free, painterly treatment.

The rhetorical amalgam of borrowings from antiquity and the Old Masters, above all from the *Laocoön* and a *Hercules on the Funeral Pyre* by Guido Reni, appealed to many of Morse's contemporaries, and *The Dying Hercules* achieved critical success. In May, 1813, the Royal Academy exhibition opened at Somerset House, and Morse found his "great picture" not only received but occupying "one of the finest places in the rooms. It has been spoken of in the papers, which you must know is considered a great compliment; for a young artist, unless extraordinary, is seldom or never mentioned till he has exhibited several times. They not only praise me, but place my picture among the most attractive in the exhibition. This I know will give you pleasure." In the same letter of June 13, 1813, he announces that he is sending home "the little cast of the Hercules which

[ALEXIS?] CHATAIGNER AFTER
MME. ANTHONY PLANTOU
*Peace of Ghent 1814 and Triumph
of America*

1814. Engraving, 14 x 16¾"
The Library Company of Philadelphia

*All the trappings of the ancient Roman
triumphal entry are introduced: obelisk,
temple, chariot, and triumphal arch.*

obtained the . . . gold medal" in sculpture for a single figure from the Society of Arts.

The phrase "unless extraordinary" is a nice touch. In the glow of his double success, Morse justifiably indulged in some transparently false modesty. To a friend: "This praise I consider much exaggerated. . . . I mention these circumstances merely to show that I am getting along as well as can be expected." To his parents: "As praise comes better from another than from one's self, I shall send you a complimentary note which Mr. West has promised to send me."

In answer to his letters and gifts, Samuel received a decidedly sharp rejoinder from his brother Richard: "Your letters . . . & also the medal gave us great pleasure. The politics however were very disagreeable & occupied no inconsiderable part of your letters. Your kind wishes for *our* reformation we must beg leave to retort by hoping for your speedy amendment. . . . Your accounts of your excursions—of your employments are what we like to hear" (November 27).

Morse's excursion of the moment was to Bristol, where he had journeyed in October, 1813, and stayed through February, 1814. The invitation had come from a rich American merchant in Bristol, Harman Visger (or Visser), whose cousin, a fellow passenger on Morse's Atlantic crossing, had introduced them. The reason for the move is clear enough from a letter written after his. visit: "I have returned from Bristol to attend the Exhibitions, and to endeavor to get a picture into Somerset House; my stay in Bristol was very pleasant indeed, as well as profitable, I was there 5 months and in May shall probably go again & stay all summer. I was getting into good business in the *portrait* way there, and if I return shall be enabled probably to support myself as long as I stay in England" (March 1). With the three years of study in England agreed to

Dorothea

1814. Etching, 5 x 3¼"
The British Museum, London

Morse made this tiny etching as a quick record of the painting that he exhibited at the Royal Academy in 1814. The subject, from Don Quixote, *was probably his first from "modern" literature. The painting itself is unlocated.*

by his father rapidly coming to a close, Morse hoped to spend a longer time abroad, which would mean supporting himself.

The picture that excited the greatest attention early that year was Allston's long-awaited *Dead Man Restored to Life*, exhibited at the recently founded British Institution. "He has obtained a wonderful share of praise for it," wrote Morse. "The picture is very deservedly ranked among the highest productions of art, either in ancient or modern times, it is really a pleasant consideration, that the palm of painting still rests with America and is, in all probability destined to remain with us" (March 14). This breathtaking conclusion is part of one of the most nationalistic letters about art that Morse ever wrote. That it was in part conditioned by the war and in part by his own recent successes seems certain.

Not so coincidentally, this letter praising Allston to the heavens preceded by only eleven days a letter from Allston to Jedidiah Morse, surely at the urging of Samuel, in support of extended study in England.

I have no hesitation in saying that his return home at present would be of the greatest disadvantage to him; having arrived just at that stage of his art when, as he is most capable of appreciating their excellence, his studying the works of the Old Masters is the most necessary. . . . Should he be obliged to return now to America, I much fear that which he has acquired would be rendered abortive. It is true he could there paint very good portraits, but I should grieve to hear at any future period that on the foundation now laid, he shall have been able to raise no higher superstructure than the fame of a portrait painter. I do not intend here any disrespect to portrait painting: I know it requires no common talent to excel in it. His model of the dying Hercules, which I suppose you have already received, will make any thing more that I can say in favour of your son's genius appear superfluous.

Six weeks later Morse added a long letter of his own, echoing these sentiments and asserting that "I shall endeavor to stay at all risks. . . . For I cannot be happy unless I am pursuing the intellectual branch of the art. Portraits have none of it; landscape has some of it, but history has it wholly." Thus in early 1814 the psychological die was cast. Morse had adopted Allston's aesthetic credo without reservation. He saw himself as a history painter, and always would, though circumstances were to dictate otherwise.

That his finest talent was for portraiture, and that only portraiture would find a ready market in the America whose artistic primacy he championed, were facts he would not accept or at least not bend to. Though there would be later crises in his artistic career, the spring of 1814 was the true turning point, because it was then that he committed himself irrevocably to inevitable frustration as a painter.

The frustration was felt all too soon. Before returning to Bristol that summer, preceded by Allston, Morse found that his cast of the *Hercules*, thought to have arrived in Charlestown by then, was still at Liverpool. An attempt to have his "great picture" taken to America also failed. "It seems as though it is destined that nothing of mine shall reach you." Then Bristol, the second time around, offered nothing but "six months' perfect neglect." His attitude toward the city and its people changed accordingly. He now perceived a "total want of anything like partiality for the fine arts in that place; the people there are but a remove from brutes. A 'Bristol hog' is as proverbial in this country as a 'Charlestown gentleman' is in Boston. . . . I have had the mortification to leave [without] a single commission. . . . I have been immured in the paralyzing atmosphere of trade till my mind was near partaking the infection. . . . I am ashamed of myself; no, never will I degrade myself by making a trade of a profession. If I cannot live a gentleman, I will starve a gentleman." These choice bits from a steaming letter of December 22, 1814, give the measure of Morse's newfound intransigence.

While in Bristol, Morse had learned that his parents would allow him to stay in Europe another year. In the meantime he had written requesting permission to travel to Paris, but got no reply. Morse's allowance was received through an American agent in London, Henry Bromfield, whom he consulted about his Paris plans. "Mr. Bromfield thinks I had better wait until I receive positive leave from you to go to France. Do write me soon and do give me leave. I long to bury myself in the Louvre in a country at least not hostile to mine. . . ." (October 11).

It was not to be. When, early in 1815, a letter arrived, it discouraged but did not prohibit the trip. Indeed, in a March letter his mother asks him to bring fabric for clothing back from Paris! But, as he wrote in reply, "*I am not there.* . . . I had not leave from you to go . . . thus letting an opportunity slip which is irrecoverable." It would be fifteen years before he would at last bury himself in the Louvre.

He began making plans to return to America. But he embarked on one last foray in the field of history painting. For the 1815 Royal Academy competition in historical composition he painted *The Judgment of Jupiter*. By the middle of July he finished the picture, modest in size but complex in the interaction of four figures. Although the decision would not be made until December, and Morse was sailing for America in August, West and Henry Fuseli—both prominent officials of the Academy—had seconded his petition to the institution to waive the rule requiring the artist's presence should he be awarded the prize. The request was refused, and Fuseli protested vigorously, to no avail. West advised Morse to stay, but he was obliged to return, taking the picture with him.

The praise of West and Fuseli can be understood in terms of the esteem then enjoyed by John Flaxman's pure line drawings, an extreme Neoclassicism derived from Greek vase paintings. The strong contours and flat, linear scheme of Morse's picture reflect that influence as well as his determination to present a moral with ideogrammatic concision. The interesting palette is dominated by light red (Apollo), rose, mauve, and dusty plum (Jupiter), and enlivened by an unusual pale yellow to cream in Marpessa's gown and her auburn hair.

Although the subject appears fleetingly in the *Iliad*, the complete story is told by Apollodorus of Carystus, a Greek poet of the third century B.C., from whom Morse derived his own description:

Apollo falls in love with Marpessa, the beautiful wife of Idas, the warrior, and elopes with her. Idas pursues them armed with bow and arrows, determined on revenge; he overtakes the lovers and is arrested in his revenge by the interference of Jupiter, who, to prevent bloodshed, gives Marpessa her choice, whether to remain with Apollo, or return to her husband. She chooses the latter, and throws herself into the arms of her husband. *This is the moment chosen. Jupiter in the cloud, accompanied by his eagle, with his hand extended over the parties, is pronouncing judgment. Marpessa, with an expression of compunction and shame, imploring forgiveness, is throwing herself into the arms of her husband. Idas, who tenderly loved Marpessa, is eagerly rushing forward to receive her, while Apollo stares with surprise and chagrin at the unexpectedness of her decision.*

When we consider that Idas is a mortal who dares physically challenge a god, that Apollo was a frequent surrogate for the king of England, and that Marpessa is conspicuously modeled on a Nike or Victory relief, the moral emerges. Victory, momentarily possessed by England, chooses to return to the brave and righteous arms of America, and does so "imploring forgiveness"! Paul J. Staiti has pointed out that the ancient sources say nothing of guilt or shame, and that this is the Calvinist inflection of Morse. And, we may add, he has given it a specifically political twist. Such symbolic interpretations of classical subject matter were habitual among painters between about 1760 and 1850.

When Morse's mother wrote to him at the end of 1814, she suggested that he had been "falling off" in economy and industry, adding pointedly: "You must not expect to paint anything in this country, for which you will receive any money to support you, but portraits; therefore do everything in your power to qualify you for painting and taking them in the best style. That is all your hope here." His first response (April 23) spoke of his rising at five and drawing from the Elgin Marbles at Burlington House for three hours, or painting in the open air before breakfast "to study the morning effect on the landscape."

About painting portraits he held his tongue for a while, undoubtedly to better control it, then wrote (May 3) with remarkable equanimity only lightly tinged with irony: "The moment I get home I wish to begin work, so that I should like to have some portraits bespoken in season. I shall charge forty dollars less than Stuart for my portraits, so that, if any of my good friends are ready, I will begin the moment I have said 'how do ye do' to them." But he makes it clear that it will be only a temporary situation: "Had I no higher thoughts than being a first-rate portrait-painter, I would have chosen a far different profession."

The London years are the most problematic of Morse's career as an artist. He received an introduction to the great art of the past, which broadened his understanding. He was indoctrinated with the tenets of the academic "great style" even as it was in decline, fixing forever his artistic ambitions. In politics he became an ardent republican whose jaundiced view of European institutions and peoples only narrowed with age. Many of the paintings made in England, especially landscapes and portraits, have disappeared, and we are left primarily with the heroic pictures in the grand manner, which are not at all typical of the oeuvre by which Morse would eventually be judged. It is a period demanding the closest attention.

Morse left England on August 21, 1815, and after a storm-tossed crossing of fifty-eight days reached landfall at Cape Cod at half-past seven in the evening, October 18. "Heaven be praised!" At eleven o'clock, "Boston Light in sight." At one o'clock, "HOME!!!"

The Judgment of Jupiter

1815. Oil on canvas, 50 x 40¼"
Yale University Art Gallery,
New Haven, Connecticut
Gift of Russell Colgate

The ancient sculptural sources of the figures proclaim themselves forthrightly. The Apollo Belvedere *for Apollo is the best known. Marpessa derives from various Nike figures, the Idas from* Menelaos with the Body of Patroclus *(popularly called* Pasquino*), and the head of Jupiter from many antique prototypes.*

The Judgment of Jupiter

III. *"Mr. Morse, from Boston"*

ALTHOUGH HE COULD NOT KNOW IT, Morse had already been accorded his first critical acclaim in America before reaching home. Jedidiah, perhaps to welcome his son, had rented a room in Boston to exhibit both the painting and the sculpture of *The Dying Hercules*, which had preceded him, and both were warmly applauded. In the *North-American Review* for September, 1815, a lengthy and astute notice appeared, even as the painter was experiencing the terror of tremendous gales at sea.

A painting by Mr. Morse, a young artist, who went from this country to England, two or three years since, is now exposed to the publick, at Mr. Greenwood's room in Tremont street. This picture is calculated to raise the highest hopes of the future celebrity of this youthful painter. . . . We do not recollect ever to have seen any figure of Hercules otherwise than in a state of repose, except . . . by Canova . . . in which he is represented, as furious, precipitating his friend Lichas into the sea. Mr. Morse has treated him after this event, and when he was expiring in agony. It was a bold attempt in a young man to represent this situation, and if it had failed, it would have hardly been discouraging; but to succeed as he has done . . . justly affords the strongest expectations of his future success. The model from which this picture was painted, obtained him a medal from the society of arts, which he most certainly merited. There are very few artists in London . . . who can execute such a model. . . . The picture is not calculated to please so much as the cast, because it is seen in a different point, and the foreshortening of the face, which is an admirable proof of skill, is not suited to please common visitors. . . . We hope by the time Mr. Morse may have completed his studies that the dormant power of patronage in the country will be awakened, and that we shall be able to keep at least one of our artists from the necessity of seeking foreign patronage.

Unhappily, such praise was not matched by public enthusiasm, and the exhibition had to be closed before Morse was even able to see it. Thus, also without his knowledge, he had suffered his first rejection by American patronage, still "dormant."

Within two months of his return, however, he opened a studio on Boston's Cornhill Square and again placed on display the *Hercules*, with some of his other works. An advertisement for "MORSE'S EXHIBITION OF PICTURES" ran in the *Recorder*, his brother Sidney's recently founded religious weekly paper. This exhibition was no more successful than the first in attracting clients. Moreover, there seem to have been no portrait commissions arranged for Morse in advance of his return. The solicitation from Joseph Delaplaine of Philadelphia in early

Elizabeth Ann Breese Morse

1816. Oil on canvas mounted on wood, 30¼ x 25⅛″
Yale University Art Gallery, New Haven, Connecticut
Gift of Richard C. Morse

While in England, Morse must have become acquainted with the paintings of Joseph Wright of Derby (1734–1797), whose fascination with artificial light sources in his portraits and subject pictures is the chief characteristic of his art. In Morse's painting, candlelight perfectly conveys the absorption of his mother (c. 1765/66–1828), serious but not dour, in her Bible.

Elizabeth Ann Breese Morse

John Adams

1816. Oil on canvas, 30 x 25"
The Brooklyn Museum
Gift of Miss Harriet H. White

To Abigail Adams's eyes, this portrait was "stern, unpleasing." The harsh, analytical probing of the face is disquieting to the viewer.

December, 1815, for two life portraits and one copy of a Copley, to be used as models for the engravings in his projected "Delaplaine's Repository of the Lives and Portraits of Distinguished American Characters," must therefore have been welcome, despite the offer of only twenty-five dollars for each—half of Morse's announced fee.

Of these commissions the 1816 portrait of John Adams is so startling that it demands attention. It is unlikely that Adams would have agreed to sit for Morse without the intervention of Jedidiah Morse. The unswerving Federalism of his father, so often assailed by the son, stood Samuel in good stead now. Adams, whose impatience extended particularly to portrait sittings, wrote good-naturedly to the elder Morse, "If your son had proposed it, I would have written him a letter too ludicrous for you to read, describing the Portraits and Busts which have already transmitted me to Posterity."

As a record of the physical decline and lingering bitterness of the eighty-one-year-old Adams, the portrait is utterly unsparing and disconcertingly objective. So inappropriate did Delaplaine deem the portrait for his gallery of "distinguished characters" that he falsely claimed that the painting had been "universally disapproved" by artists and others who had seen it, going so far as to "quote" from a fictitious letter by an anonymous critic.

The image is at such a distance from the idealizing portraits of Morse's London experience that we are hard put to explain the abrupt transition. It is possible that the memorable portrait of Benjamin West painted by Allston in 1814, equally revealing of age and infirmity, was in Morse's mind. But it may also be that his return to New England, where colonial portraiture was once again before his eyes, played a role. Perhaps he sensed that an old rebel should be painted like an old rebel, in the style of his youth and first celebrity. Perhaps, on more specifically stylistic grounds, Morse was also trying to come to terms with that basic American portrait manner of descriptive realism whose highest exponent had been John Singleton Copley. Copley, whose portrait of John Hancock Morse was copying for Delaplaine, had worked assiduously in a linear manner. This is recalled in Morse's angular drawing of Adams's right eye, with its multiple lines and folds, as well as in the sharply designed contour of his coat collar and lapel. Even the pink and red shadows that model the face are applied in a linear fashion. In its homeliness, however, the *John Adams* is suggestive of the itinerant portrait tradition in colonial and federal America, which Samuel Morse would soon reluctantly continue.

In that remarkable letter of March 14, 1814, in which Morse had claimed the "palm of painting" for America, he had continued: "All we wish is *a taste* in the country, and a little more *wealth*; taste is altogether acquired . . . any man of good common sense . . . may in a short time become a man of taste. . . . In order to create a taste, however, pictures, first-rate pictures, must be introduced into the country. . . ." He had then praised the establishment of America's first art academy, the Pennsylvania Academy of the Fine Arts in Philadelphia, and urged, "Let every American feel a pride in supporting that Institution, let it be a *national* not a *city* business."

He was proud when the Pennsylvania Academy decided to purchase Allston's *Dead Man Restored*; after hearing the news, he sent his own *Hercules* painting in May, 1816, to the Academy's annual exhibition. Again, it was praised, with a critic citing it as "another gratifying evidence of American genius. . . . Philadelphia may be proud that her academy contains at the same moment, the reviving man of *Allston*, and the *Dying Hercules* of *Morse*." Unsold, his painting returned to Boston.

At home, in lieu of commissions, Morse painted family portraits during the spring and summer. His grandfather, father, mother, and brothers sat to him, and he treated each with a clear attempt at appropriate characterization. The portrait of Elizabeth Ann Breese Morse, popularly called *By Candlelight*, balances formal strength with a glow of maternal intimacy, owed primarily to the poetry of the light from the unseen candle. The effects of transparency in the lace bodice, collar, and bonnet enhance the painting's charm.

FOLLOWING PAGES

Elizabeth Kneeland McFarland

c. 1816. Oil on millboard, 11⅞ x 10"
Private collection

Five months before Morse's arrival in Concord, Mrs. McFarland (1780–1838) had written in her diary for March 19, "My birth-day! O, what contrition and shame have I felt to-day. . . . Have I lived so long and done nothing for God? O why did I not improve the season of youth to more advantage? . . . Where am I? and to what kingdom do I belong? . . . There must be some wrong in me that my hopes are constantly mingled with so much doubting."

Reverend Asa McFarland

c. 1816. Oil on millboard, 11⅞ x 10"
Private collection

Of Asa McFarland (1769/70–1827), his son wrote: "I have a very clear recollection of a scowl which gathered upon the face of my father at the dinner-table on a convention day. There was some carving to be done, and he invited a notoriously lazy clergyman of Hillsborough county to assist. He was a large and apparently robust man, but excused himself 'because his wrists were weak.' "

Elizabeth Kneeland McFarland

Reverend Asa McFarland

Samuel Sparhawk

c. 1816. Oil on millboard, 12 x 9⅞"
New Hampshire Historical Society, Concord

Sparhawk (1777–1834) was a second cousin by marriage to Lucretia Pickering Walker Morse. Among the many favors he did for Samuel Morse was his assistance in the sale of the Morse brothers' fire-engine pump to the town of Concord.

Since no commissions were forthcoming in Boston and Charlestown, Morse headed north to Concord, New Hampshire, in August, 1816, bearing letters of introduction to his father's fellow clergymen and others. The first of these pastoral friends to be visited was the Reverend Asa McFarland and his third wife, Elizabeth. Their son, Asa, later pasted handwritten labels on the backs of the portraits of his parents, which give 1818 as the date of execution. But in his 1880 memoirs, although uncertain of the date of Morse's arrival, McFarland observed, "My parents were, I think, the first subjects of his pencil; and the habitation in which they dwelt was his studio." The hospitality they extended to Samuel was habitual. "The position of father as the only ordained clergyman in Concord . . . caused his dwelling to be the resort not merely of his brethren in the ministry, but of their wives and children. This sometimes became an infliction, because even clergymen have not always a sense of propriety. . . . My parents were more patient than could properly have been expected, especially my mother, who probably entertained the belief that angels could come in the guise of even uncouth clergymen."

These remarkable portraits, still owned by descendants of the sitters, again bear witness to the pronounced shift in the artist's style when confronted with representatives of the vigorous and rigorous New England clergy in whose intellectual and moral sphere he had been raised. Rectitude is enthroned in these visages, and piety, too. In Asa McFarland's face, intelligence is combined with a properly skeptical directness, warmth with reserve. Intelligence also marks his wife's head, but in the large staring eyes doubt seems mingled with revelation. The startling absence of light in her eyes is a tiny detail that conveys her otherworldly longings.

Perhaps these paintings were gifts to the McFarlands for their hospitality. Certainly, through them, Morse was quickly able to attract clients. Working swiftly in a small format, by August 16 he had completed five "at fifteen dollars each and have two more engaged and many more talked of." The low price reflected the relative lack of esteem with which the local gentry were accustomed to regard an artist. It was a far cry from the elevated plane Morse had known in England. Still, his talents were far above the New Hampshire norm, and he believed he could make a fortune *if* he were to be a portraitist solely, "so great is the desire for good portraits in the different country towns."

Fifteen dollars could command no more than a small cabinet portrait on millboard, similar to those of the McFarlands. But these could be painted much more rapidly than a larger picture, not just because of the size but also because the surface required less attention to organization and accessories. A neutral background, the hint of a chair, a half-length pose omitting the hands were all that was needed, and the artist could concentrate on the face—that which above all interested his Concord sitters.

He soon met Samuel Sparhawk, thirty-nine years old and secretary of state of New Hampshire as well as cashier at Concord's Upper Bank. Sparhawk, "very much my friend," invited Morse to dinner within those first two weeks in Con-

Reverend Nathan Parker

1817. Oil on millboard, c. 10 x 8″
Andover Hall, Harvard Divinity School,
Cambridge, Massachusetts

*In 1819 Dr. Parker (1782–1833) went
to Baltimore for the ordination of Jared
Sparks. It was on this occasion that William Ellery Channing definitively proclaimed the doctrines of Unitarianism,
formalizing the split within Congregationalism that had bitterly obsessed
Morse's father for twenty-five years. Although Parker was censured as an infidel
by the Pascataqua Association of Minis-
ters, he remained pastor of the South Par-
ish until his death.*

cord, and there he met Lucretia Pickering Walker. Morse was immediately attracted to her, writing to his parents that he flattered himself he "might be a
successful suitor," adding that "there is still no need of hurry; the young lady is
but sixteen." Probably about this time he took Sparhawk's lanky likeness, memorable for its sloping pose and the pensive minor key that it strikes. Again we see
Morse's propensity for capturing the essence within the likeness and his solid
technique, incisive rather than flashy. Also of note is the economy of his means;
here, for example, the subtly modulated contour of Sparhawk's face lends a note
of poetry to the natural shrewdness of his features.

On September 3 Morse left Concord—temporarily, for he and Lucretia
were already engaged!—to search out other markets for his talents. The Concord commissions had dried up for the moment; he had completed six portraits
at fifteen dollars and one at ten dollars (for the last person had "obtained four of

my sitters for me"). He went to Hanover, then on to Walpole, where he met "with no success. . . . *Quacks* have been here before me." However, he stayed more than three weeks and business picked up. "I am doing pretty well in this place, better than I expected; I have one more portrait to do before I leave it." He painted seven at Windsor, as he had done at Concord.

Still he dreamed of grander projects. Dartmouth College was in the midst of a great crisis, soon to have more than statewide significance. The college trustees, Federalists all, had recently fired the president, John Wheelock, who had then enlisted the aid of the Democrat-controlled state legislature to declare the private college a public university (with himself as president). The college sued, and in a famous argument Daniel Webster persuaded the Supreme Court under Chief Justice John Marshall that the college charter was a contract with the state that could not be violated—a decision (1819) of historic importance.

Morse wrote to his parents (September 28) of an idea "which has just come into my head: that of sending to you for my great canvas and painting the quarrel at Dartmouth College, as large as life, with all the portraits of the trustees, overseers, officers of college, and students"; he proposed "to ask five thousand dollars for it. . . . Is it not a grand scheme?" This project, which never got beyond the imagining of it, is noteworthy because it again reveals the kind of "grand" subject that attracted Morse. Like the *Marius*, the *Hercules*, and the *Judgment of Jupiter*, his "Dartmouth Quarrel" would have been symbolic, significant, static—an image that appealed to the intellectual and moral faculties rather than to the emotions.

It is also interesting because Morse turned to a contemporary American event, tacitly admitting that the European pantheon of historical and mythological subjects could not be naturalized. That it was to be, however, what West had called "a ten acre picture" is clear. Morse proposed to use "my great canvas," which he had brought home from England for whatever heroic project might arise. This is the canvas of which half would soon serve for his 1822 painting of *The House of Representatives*. Though he returned to Hanover at the beginning of October, 1816, his "grand scheme" is not mentioned again.

By the middle of the month Morse was back in Concord to inform Lucretia's parents of their engagement. Despite his "dread of being an old bachelor" (he was now twenty-five!), he was uncharacteristically diffident in approaching them. In September his father had urged him to acquaint the Walkers "with the state of the business, as she is so young and the thing so important to them." And his mother had reminded him that "there are a great many etcs., etcs., that we want to know. . . . You see your mother has not lived twenty-seven years in New England without learning to ask questions." The Walkers, probably wondering what had taken him so long, gave the match their " 'entire approbation.' Everything successful!"

After spending November and early December at home in Charlestown, Morse went on the road again before Christmas. December 14 found him in Portsmouth, New Hampshire: "I should have written you sooner but I have been employed in settling myself. . . . I have taken lodgings and a room at Mrs. Rindge's in Jaffrey Street; a very excellent and central situation. . . . I shall com-

Lucretia Pickering Walker Morse

c. 1818. Chalk crayons on paper, 12 x 9⅜"
New Hampshire Historical Society, Concord

Done in Charleston, South Carolina, soon after Morse's marriage to Lucretia, this gentle drawing remained in her family until 1979. Black-and-white chalks are used skillfully over the natural light-brown ground of the paper. Red chalk lends emphasis to her features and to the ornamental bows on her dress.

MR. MORSE, FROM BOSTON

Lucretia Pickering Walker Morse

Mrs. Joseph Orne

1817. Oil on millboard, 12 x 10″
Trustees of the Ropes Memorial,
Salem, Massachusetts

Sally Ropes (1795–1876) married her cousin Joseph Orne (1796–1818) in May, 1817, and moved into the Ropes family home in Salem in September, one month after Morse painted their portraits, which have hung there ever since.

mence on Monday morning with Governor Langdon's portrait. He is very kind and attentive to me, as, indeed, are all here, and will do everything to aid me." The Langdon portrait has resisted identification among the known likenesses of the seventy-five-year-old former governor, but the commission certainly suggests that Morse's reputation had preceded him to Portsmouth.

Early in 1817, Lucretia came to Portsmouth to visit relatives, at least one of whom was painted by Morse. This was the Reverend Nathan Parker, who in 1815 had married Susan Pickering, Lucretia's aunt. Graduated from Harvard in 1803, he then studied theology and was ordained minister at South Church, Portsmouth, in 1808. A modest, pleasant man whose sensible sermons proceeded from his habit of writing them as if they were letters, Parker was treated by Morse to a somewhat elaborate setting and an inventive palette despite the

MR. MORSE, FROM BOSTON

Orne's account book survives. For August 19, 1817, it records, "By Mr. Morse for painting Likenesses 40.00," and for November 1, "By S. Lathrop for 2 gilt frames/7.00." He graduated at the head of his Harvard Divinity class the next spring and died in September at twenty-two.

portrait's small size. Dressed in ecclesiastical black, he sits in a turquoise-upholstered chair with gilt molding, framed by red drapery. His genial expression is seconded by the pose, a casual variation on Morse's accustomed Concord formula. Unhappily, this painting, perhaps alone among Morse's work, suggests that he included bitumen among his pigments. The curdled black surface of the coat and hair, and the subsequent loss of modeling in those passages, is symptomatic of the problems caused by this asphaltum, which was especially popular among English painters of the eighteenth century.

In late January or early February Lucretia accompanied Samuel to Charlestown to meet his parents. He then returned to Portsmouth, where he soon found "a *press of business*. I shall have three begun to-night; one sat yesterday (a large one), and two will sit to-day (small), and three more have it in serious contemplation" (March 4). "The unexpected application of three sitters at a time completely stopped me. Since I wrote I have taken a first sitting of a fourth (large), and a fifth (large) sits on Friday morning; so you see I am over head and ears in business" (March 5).

Despite his Portsmouth success, Morse was still unhappy in the portrait business. He was soon back in Boston, looking for ways to make enough money so that he might marry Lucretia. Painting was neglected that spring and summer while he and his brother Sidney designed and built an improved flexible-piston pump for use in "gardens and streets," which they fondly hoped would also prove useful to fire departments. One fire-engine pump was ordered for Concord, New Hampshire, but it failed to work. Still, a model pump that Samuel showed to his former professors at Yale, Benjamin Silliman and Jeremiah Day, earned their praise. About the same time the brothers designed a system of propelling a steamboat "by action on a column of water." They described the project to a captain at the Charlestown Navy Yard on April 2, 1817, but it was not carried further.

Much more surprising was Samuel's sudden strong desire to prepare for the ministry. His parents, perhaps thinking of the expensive years in London, talked him out of this belated enthusiasm.

There were some portrait commissions that summer. He probably took the pensive likenesses of the newlyweds Joseph and Sally Orne in Charlestown, for Joseph was a divinity student at Harvard. As usual, Morse posed his sitters on fashionable Empire side chairs of the klismos type known from Greek vases. He may have had Samuel Sparhawk to thank for the commission, as Sparhawk and Sally were cousins.

Still closer to home, he painted Jeremiah Evarts, who with Morse's father edited the *Panoplist*, a Calvinist monthly paper. This splendid, penetrating portrait communicates the strong will and uncompromising intellect for which Evarts was known. It could indeed be subtitled "The Panoplist," which signifies the invincible or full-armored man, with reference in the religious sphere to Ephesians 6:11–17, especially, "Put on the whole armor of God, that ye may be able to stand against the wiles of the devil." It is fascinating to compare this portrait with

Jeremiah Evarts

1817. Oil on canvas, 30¼ x 25"
From the Collection of Charles Hosmer Morse
Museum of American Art,
Winter Park, Florida,
through the courtesy of the
Charles Hosmer Morse Foundation

One of the most brilliant members of the "unusually brilliant" Yale class of 1802, Evarts (1781–1831) first tried the practice of law but, in the opinion of a contemporary, "ever had too much unbending integrity to be a popular lawyer." Eloquent and principled, he was a founder and officer of the American Board of Commissioners for Foreign Missions. In this capacity he became aware of the condition of the Indian tribes east of the Mississippi and, together with Jedidiah Morse, fought against the outrage of their forcible removal to reservations in the West.

Jeremiah Evarts

General John Stark

1817. Oil on panel, 20 x 16"
American Scenic and Historic
Preservation Society
Philipse Manor State Historic Site,
Yonkers, New York

*This striking study seems to reflect Gilbert
Stuart's injunction, as recorded by Matthew Jouett, "that in the commencement of
all portraits the first idea is an indistinct
mass of light and shadows."*

those of Samuel Sparhawk and Jedidiah Morse, as recorded and interpreted by
Samuel Morse. All the heads are quite similar in shape and structure, yet the
comfortable slouch of the dispassionate bank cashier is far removed from the literal uprightness of the two Calvinists.

Among the most interesting commissions of 1817 is the puzzling portrait of
the Revolutionary War hero General John Stark. The only record, if such it may
be called, concerning this painting is in a letter from Lucretia in Concord to Samuel in Portsmouth (December 29, 1816): "Mr. Stark is coming to Boston soon and
intends to see you." It cannot refer to the eighty-nine-year-old general, who was
housebound and senile in Manchester, New Hampshire.

Paul J. Staiti has concluded that Major Caleb Stark, the general's middle-
aged son, who was said to bear a strong resemblance to him, must have come to
Boston as a surrogate for his father. The uniform here is of a general of the War

of 1812, although Caleb never attained a higher rank than major in that conflict. Thus the uniform must have been borrowed or rented by Morse to complete the painting. John Stark's grandson, also named Caleb, in his edition of the *Memoirs of General John Stark* (1860), observed that "the portrait of Major Stark by S.F.B. Morse resembles the General more than [the anonymous engraving] at the head of this volume." That is to say, he was aware that his father had posed for the "portrait" of his grandfather.

Providing further, tangible support for this hypothesis is the existence of a smaller panel painting of John Stark that has every appearance of being the life study of Caleb Stark. This work, in which the uniform plays little part, accentuates the structure of the head and drops the eyes into even deeper shadow than they are in the large formal portrait. This life study is essentially a mask, precisely what one would expect in the supposed circumstances. Morse sought the basic family resemblance between son and father, then aged the features and brought out the eyes slightly. This commission may also have been owed to Samuel Sparhawk, whose sister-in-law was Major Caleb Stark's wife.

In the larger painting, both the high flesh tones and the general conception of a military portrait derive from Gilbert Stuart, whose influence on Morse first becomes noticeable in 1817. But the casual, sometimes superficial, charm that marks Stuart's sitters was largely alien to Morse. Although he increasingly experimented with Stuart's palette, and his brushwork became more supple, he usually invested his sitters with a degree of New England reserve that contrasts with Stuart's more casual, conversational attitudes. Even when he adopted the languorous, fluent poses of Thomas Sully for some of his Charleston portraits, Morse edged them with a scarcely perceptible hint of unease or invested the pose with greater urgency. In short, he preferred character to attitude.

Although his price for a small portrait may have increased from fifteen to twenty dollars, Samuel needed money to marry. There were not only Morse connections but also relatives of Washington Allston in South Carolina. He had been told artists were held in higher esteem in the aristocratic South and were paid higher prices in that flourishing economy. Late in 1817, he accepted an invitation to South Carolina extended by James E. B. Finley, who lived in Charleston.

It seemed as if he would never be ready to leave: "Portraits and engines, and pumps and bellows, and various models of various things, letters to write, and visits to pay, and preparations for voyages by sea and land, all crowd upon me." After a stop in New Haven, and a visit to John Trumbull's studio in New York City, Morse journeyed on to Charleston, arriving there on January 27, 1818. It was indeed a more halcyon climate than he was accustomed to, in both patronage and temperature. "I think my prospects are favorable."

General John Stark

1817. Oil on canvas, 29⅞ x 25″
Oak Ridge Collection,
on loan to the White House

After service in the Seven Years' War, Stark (1728–1822) fought as a colonel at Bunker Hill and with Washington in New Jersey during the winter of 1776–77. Later in 1777 he was made a brigadier general of a militia force near Bennington, Vermont, where he defeated two units of Burgoyne's army. He was rewarded with the commission of brigadier general in the Continental Army and in 1783 promoted to major general.

IV. "I Migrate to Charleston"

Dr. Alexander Baron

1818. Oil on canvas, 29 x 25"
Courtesy of the Medical Society of South
Carolina, Charleston

The genial touch of informality bestowed by the spectacles pushed up on Baron's forehead has a precedent in the post-humous 1813 portrait of his Edinburgh classmate, Dr. Benjamin Rush, by Thomas Sully (private collection, on loan to the National Museum of American Art). This vivid portrait of Baron (1745–1819) commemorated his presidency of the St. Andrew's Society of Charleston.

Dr. James E. B. Finley

1818. Oil on canvas, 30 x 25"
Copyright © Indianapolis Museum of Art.
Gift of Mrs. E. Vernon Hahn.

"Your pictures—aye—suppose I should speak of them and what is said of them during your absence. I will perform the office of him who was placed near the triumphal car of the conqueror to abuse him lest he should be too elated.... 'See,' say others, 'how he flatters.' 'Oh!' says another, 'he has not flattered me' " (Dr. Finley to Morse, June 16, 1818).

FINLEY, I AM AFRAID YOU WILL BE TOO HAPPY," wrote Dr. Finley to his grandnephew in June, 1818, following Morse's first winter in Charleston. "You ought to meet a little rub or two or you will be too much in the clouds and forget that you are among mortals."

That first season in the sun had been a grand success for Morse, as this affectionate gibe suggests. It had begun poorly. According to Dunlap, there was no interest in the visiting painter for weeks. " 'This will not do, sir,' he said to the Doctor, 'I must ask you to permit me to paint your portrait as a remembrance, and I will go home again.' " Success followed his portrait of Dr. Finley, which was so greatly admired that it generated a spate of commissions. It is reported that within a few weeks Morse had about one hundred fifty subscriptions. From his own list of portraits commissioned in Charleston that winter, we find that he began at least fifty-three (in addition to that of his uncle) during the four months he remained in the city. Some of the portraits, especially the more elaborate ones, were taken north to be finished in the summer, but he completed enough work—Dunlap says four a week—at an average fee of nearly eighty dollars to amass several thousand dollars by June, and he was ready to marry.

One of Dr. Finley's fellow physicians, Dr. Alexander Baron, was among the first to engage a portrait, and it is among the most memorable. Morse concerned himself solely with the forthright expression of character and intelligence. He effectively combines the stability of a fully frontal head with a suggestion of the transient moment, as though Baron had turned from reading a letter in response to the viewer's presence. The hand, so rare in Morse's work until now, gives a second point of compositional interest helpful in the larger format that now became more frequent.

The June letter from Uncle Finley, as Morse called him, had continued: "By the bye, I saw old General C. C. Pinckney yesterday, and he told me, in his laughing, humorous way, that he had requested you to draw his brother Thomas twenty years younger than he really was, so as to be a companion to his own when he was twenty years younger . . . and to flatter him as he had directed Stuart to do so to him." Since Charles Cotesworth Pinckney paid Morse three hundred dollars for the portrait of General Thomas Pinckney, a little flattery would not have been out of place. Certainly the painting is idealized in the Stuart manner, with brilliant colors, a sweeping curtain, and the swirling clouds of an imaginary sky. Morse did not follow the facetious suggestion to restore the general's youth; per-

Dr. James E. B. Finley

General Thomas Pinckney

1818. Oil on canvas, 43 x 38″
Anonymous loan to The Columbia Museum of
Art, South Carolina

Educated in England and France, Pinckney (1750–1828) served in the Revolutionary War and was a major general in command of the Southeast during the War of 1812. In his civilian career he was governor and U.S. minister to Great Britain. He negotiated the treaty that set the boundaries between the United States and the Spanish territories in America and was the second president general of the Society of the Cincinnati, whose order he wears around his neck.

haps the memories of his attempt to *age* Major Stark were too fresh. *General Thomas Pinckney* was Morse's most elaborate portrait to date and, not surprisingly, it exposes some technical shortcomings, notably in the constrained space and the sitter's unduly short legs. These problems were resolved in his next large portrait, that of Colonel William Drayton.

Delivered to the colonel in the fall, the commission was probably occasioned by Drayton's appointment as President James Monroe's secretary of war. The self-conscious stiffness of the sitter suggests such a weighty occasion. The imposing open folio has not yet been identified but is probably significant. Certainly this is true of the columns and entablature seen through the window. Rather too monumental, not to mention nonfunctional, even for the antebellum South, they must be understood emblematically as a reminder of the Roman foundations of the new republic and of Drayton's prominence in the law, the military, and the government of that republic. It exemplifies the grand-manner portrait, which testifies to the dignity of the sitter through association with the classical past. The architecture here is so specifically rendered that its inspiration may lie in prints of English portraits, perhaps even in the work of Benjamin West.

As his uncle had surmised, the summer and autumn in Charlestown and Concord must have been one of the most satisfying periods of Morse's life. His ego and his pocketbook were healthy, he had satisfying work to do, and marriage to Lucretia would crown these charmed months. Something of his sense of his own worth may be seen in the romantically charged *Self-Portrait*, which was very likely done at about the time of his wedding. While small in size like his other New England portraits, it is not on millboard. For himself he reserved a fine wood panel. Moreover, the scale is different, with the head dominant. One might surmise that the elegant coat with gray-black neckcloth was his wedding outfit. The expressive vitality of the pensive head extends to the painterly gray background, streaked with light brown and darker gray. It seems an easy matter to read this face. Intense, inward, and sensual, with an overall aura of youthful purpose and determination, it is a memorable record of the rising artist and new husband.

The wedding was in Concord on September 29, 1818. The notice in the *Patriot* informed the community: "Married in this town by Rev. Dr. McFarland, Mr. Samuel F. B. Morse (the celebrated painter) to Miss Lucretia Walker, daughter of Charles Walker, Esq." It was appropriate that the Reverend McFarland, his earliest supporter in Concord, should officiate, and his son, in his memoirs, summed up the encounter between Morse and Concord:

*He treated the people of this settlement, then of about twelve hundred inhabitants, to three surprises,—*first, *by portraits which could be recognized at sight, wherever exhibited;* second, *by captivating, capturing, and conveying away from town, in the face of Concord young men, a lady remarkable above all others of her sex then here for her beauty, and estimable for her excellences; and* thirdly, *by the munificence of the fee bestowed upon the clergyman who solemnized the marriage.*

In November the generous painter and his esteemed bride sailed to South Carolina, arriving in Charleston on the nineteenth and taking lodgings at Uncle Finley's, where they would remain through the winter and spring of 1819.

Consider, for a moment, the city that had so altered our painter's life. In *The American Geography*, in 1789, Jedidiah Morse had described its charm: "The refreshing sea breezes . . . render Charleston more healthy than any part of the low country in the southern states. On this account it is the resort of great numbers of gentlemen . . . who come here to spend the *sickly months*, as they are called, in quest of health and of the social enjoyments which the city affords."

The prosperity of Charleston was linked to its great harbor, from which were shipped exports of South Carolina's staple crops of rice, indigo, and, increasingly, cotton. The colonial beginnings and the names of both state and city were, of course, owed to Charles II, who had rewarded many of those who restored him to the throne with land grants in America. In the Carolinas the new owners entrusted their estates to the management of the well-established sugar planters of the West Indies. They in turn established their plantation system on the mainland and, upon finding that sugar would not grow there, they planted rice.

Increasingly, however, the port city of Charleston assumed dominance over the plantations. Its great urbanity was due in part to the desire of the English to emulate London, in part to the great numbers of industrious Huguenot artisans who emigrated from a hostile France, and in part to the intellectual vitality of its Jewish population, which by 1810 encompassed nearly half of all the Jews in America. Many of these were Sephardim, who, like the Huguenots, arrived in search of religious toleration, and found it.

All of these peoples and circumstances had created a city whose enjoyment of luxury was unsurpassed in colonial America. But those who enjoyed luxury and urbanity were supported by the labor of black slaves—fifty-one percent of the population in 1820. Although South Carolina had abolitionist societies and in fact had prohibited the slave trade between 1787 and 1803, after the War of 1812 that trade grew as the importance of King Cotton grew—by leaps and bounds. Charleston, in Carleton Mabee's memorable phrase, was a "gracious slavocracy," and her seductiveness may well have conditioned Morse's subsequent pro-slavery stance.

The Revolutionary War was for Charleston a first civil war, dividing families as well as townspeople, and this was repeated with the War of 1812. The city's fortunes went into a slow decline after independence. As cotton came to dominate all other exports and no southern banking or credit system was developed to support the trade, the Charleston that welcomed Samuel Morse with a cultured, prosperous smile was in fact approaching a crisis, though he could not have foreseen it and her citizens ignored it.

Morse resumed work on his portraits. The fine painting of Mrs. James Ladson, distinguished by an absence of flattery, probably dates from this time. The sober head and compositional restraint are heightened by contrast with the brilliant sunset sky, with its Stuart-inspired palette. Stuart's influence is more far-reaching in Morse's portraits of Martha Pawley LaBruce and her son Joseph

Colonel William Drayton

1818. Oil on canvas, 48 x 38¼"
The White House, Washington, D.C.
Gift of an anonymous donor

Lawyer, soldier, secretary of war, and four-term congressman, Drayton (1776–1846) was maligned as an opponent of John C. Calhoun's nullification doctrine. His pro-Union views earned him such enmity at home that he moved to Philadelphia. His last public position was president of the Bank of the United States, for long the center of controversy, which he ended by closing it.

Percival LaBruce. Drawing is abandoned in favor of soft massings of transparent, liquid color, and contours are merely the indistinct boundaries of these areas. In Matthew Jouett's notes on Stuart's teaching, which Morse had copied out for himself, he had read Stuart's injunction to "load your pictures, but keep your colors as separate as you can. No blending, 'tis destructive of clear and beautiful effect. . . . Drawing the features distinctly and carefully with chalk is loss of time; all studies should be made with the brush in hand."

For Morse, the happiest part of his South Carolina experience was the patronage of John Ashe Alston. A prince among patrons, he not only commissioned myriad portraits of himself and his relatives but also rewarded Morse with unparalleled generosity. Unhappily for both their posterities, most of the eighteen or so portraits have disappeared, apparently lost to fire. Portraits of Alston's parents, his half-brother, and himself are all that are now known to exist. The sorriest loss is the lifesize, full-length portrait of his frail, consumptive daughter,

Martha Pawley LaBruce

c.1819. Oil on canvas, 30 x 25"
Private collection, South Carolina

Morse achieves an unusual blend of somber meditation and painterly splendor. The silent visage of Mrs. LaBruce (1766–1822) bespeaks her widowhood as much as her black dress. Yet color is used richly throughout, in the paisley shawl and petit-point bag, in the sky, and also in the superbly modeled face.

Sally. Although she lived to be seventy-one, at the time Alston was sure she was near death and ordered no fewer than six likenesses of her.

Alston was knowledgeable about painting and had definite ideas about what he wanted in the way of pose and accessories, even suggesting works by other artists as appropriate models for Morse. He knew that painting was an art, not just a craft, and that one paid accordingly. He understood that a portrait "with hands" cost more than one without. For the lost full-length portrait of Sally, he paid Morse eight hundred dollars. It should not be forgotten that the high prices that Morse commanded in Charleston were not simply a sign of urbane taste and culture, but also an indication of the city's economic prosperity. Roger G. Kennedy (in *Architecture, Men, Women and Money*) reports that the average white Charlestonian "owned assets worth $41,650 in 1980 dollars, in contrast to an average of $12,400 in New England." Morse's fondness for southern hospitality is not surprising.

While it is disconcerting to discuss lost paintings, the importance of the portrait of Sally Alston deserves a few more words. Commissioned in January, 1819, it was taken back to Charlestown for completion, where it was seen by Washington Allston, who had returned to America for good. Allston wrote about the painting in November to Charles Robert Leslie in London: "Morse has spent the summer here and has just finished a large whole length portrait of a beautiful girl wandering amid the ruins of a gothic abbey. Tis well drawn, composed and colored, and would make a figure at Somerset House. I always thought he had a great deal in him, if he would only bring it out by application, which you will be glad to hear he at length has acquired." The poetic metaphor of the landscape setting was clearly in harmony with the rhetorical fervor of John Ashe Alston's own expressed fears: "How often shall I leave the grave of my child for the society of this picture. It shall be placed in a room where none shall enter but myself. There prostrate and alone, I shall offer you the humble tribute of my gratitude."

It would be a mistake to assume that the Gothic romanticism of the picture was totally out of character for Morse. Alston's anguish would have recalled to the artist the death in infancy of six of his own brothers and sisters, and a similar poetic strain surfaces on at least two later occasions—in the nostalgic grandeur of his portrait of Lafayette and in the hushed lyricism of the portrait of Morse's daughter, called *The Muse*.

Certainly the most prestigious commission he received in Charleston was not of a resident, but of President James Monroe, who was coming in April, 1819, to "inspect the coast defenses and make himself acquainted with the people." Since this was the first presidential visit to Charleston since Washington's, the Common Council of Charleston had resolved unanimously on March 1 that the president be requested "to permit a full-length likeness to be taken for the City of

Mrs. James Ladson

James Monroe

1820. Oil on canvas, 92½ x 59½"
Collection of City Hall, Charleston,
South Carolina

The president holds his Revolutionary War hat in his left hand, while his right is placed next to the Constitution. The splendor of the setting, much of it handsomely painted, nonetheless has the flavor of South Carolina rather than the White House. Morse never seems to have perceived the unevenness of this painting, perhaps understandably in view of the importance of the commission.

James Monroe

1819–20. Oil on canvas, 29½ x 24⅝"
The White House, Washington, D.C.
Gift of Michael Straight

Although we do not know whether it was executed in December, 1819, in Washington or in Charleston in 1820, this is presumed to be the copy of the head ordered by one of the president's daughters. The work remained in the Monroe family until the early twentieth century. It is a splendid, fluid portrait in which the vibrant flow of light and the consonant, cursive lines of the contours, eyebrows, and furrows of the face are held in dignified balance by the aloof, three-quarter pose.

Charleston, and that Mr. Morse be requested to take all necessary measures for executing the said likeness on the visit of the President to this city . . . [and] that the sum of seven hundred and fifty dollars be appropriated for this purpose."

The brevity of Monroe's stay in Charleston made sitting to Morse impossible; plans were made for the artist to go to Washington in the fall to begin work. But first he and Lucretia returned to Charlestown in the early summer. His pleasure in his growing reputation and prosperity was tempered by the news that his father was increasingly under attack from his congregation. His theological conservatism and disputatious bent brought the crisis rapidly to a head, and at the end of August he resigned his pulpit. The "Unitarian hydra," as his son styled the opposition, had prevailed at home. Despite Samuel's suggestion that his parents relocate to Charleston, in the spring they moved to the more familiar New Haven.

I MIGRATE TO CHARLESTON

Alexander Calder

c. 1820. Oil on canvas, 30 x 25"
R. Philip Hanes, Jr. Collection
Winston-Salem, North Carolina

Born in Edinburgh, Scotland, Calder (c. 1771/73–1849) was in Charleston by 1796 and in business as a cabinetmaker, advertising "a Variety of elegant and useful Cabinet Work," including "handsome Chairs and Sofas of the newest fashion.... All of which will be sold low for cash or produce." He later became a builder and owner of the fashionable Planters Hotel.

In July, 1819, Morse went some thirty miles into the country to paint the memorable likeness of the ninety-one-year-old Henry Bromfield at Harvard, Massachusetts. His daughter Sarah had married Eliphalet Pearson, the brilliant scholar who had been the Reverend Morse's ally in the struggle against the "hydra," and his son Henry, living in England, had been the agent through whom Jedidiah financed Samuel's London years. The relentless realism of this patriarchal image is that found in the finest American portrayals of old age, from Copley to Eakins and beyond. Probing the lines, textures, and colors of this venerable head, Morse's realism penetrates to the very core of age and the experiences of a lifetime. The portrait is an anatomy of ordinary heroism.

Much of the rest of the summer was devoted to the large portrait of Sally Alston, which was finished by November when Morse departed for Washington.

John Ashe Alston

c. 1819. Oil on millboard, 10 x 8"
Historic Charleston Foundation, South Carolina

The portrait of Alston (1783–1831) is based on an engraving of Gilbert Stuart's portrait of Fisher Ames published in an 1814 Analectic *Magazine and sent to Morse by Alston himself. Although poorly preserved, it is one of the few surviving works of the many commissioned by the wealthy planter.*

But painting was far from his only concern. First, there was his father's resignation; soon afterward, Lucretia gave birth to their first child, Susan Walker Morse, and would therefore be unable to return to Charleston that winter. In the meantime, Dr. Finley had died, and Morse's annual season in the South assumed a bleak aspect.

Through renewed daily contact with his beleaguered father and with Jeremiah Evarts, he was directly affected by the activities of their American Board of Commissioners for Foreign Missions, then nine years old. The only mission to date had been to India in 1813. Now two missions were launched simultaneously, one to Palestine and the other to the Sandwich Islands (Hawaii).

The latter mission was composed of seven couples. It is thought that Morse painted all of their portraits, singly or paired. Not all have been located, but lithographs after others support this assumption. For these portraits he reverted to his New England format of the small millboard, obviously because of the low price he must have been paid for each. All of them may have been painted in the month preceding the October 23 sailing of the *Thaddeus*.

The double portrait of the Reverend and Mrs. Hiram Bingham, a harsh-looking man and a homely woman, is strongly characterized, particularly in the way Mrs. Bingham's head, though placed farther back than her husband's, pushes forward inquisitively. Lest it be forgotten that missionary work had a political component, it should be noted that the Reverend Bingham urged his Boston backers to turn their attention to the Oregon Territory, which, unlike California, was still free of Mexico and Catholicism. His promptings were a significant factor in America's securing of Oregon over the next two decades.

Dr. Thomas Holman, the first medical missionary to the Islands, and his wife, Lucia Ruggles, were to remain there for only two years. Mrs. Ruggles kept a journal of the five-month, twenty-thousand-mile voyage around Cape Horn. It is a vivid record of missionary zeal and the very personal responses of a missionary's wife in "Owhyhee." Near the end of this journal, after their arrival on March 30, 1820, is a remarkable passage:

I am fully convinced that females may be useful, eminently useful to a foreign Mission; that their influence and example are everything to a Missionary establishment. . . . I believe the females of this Mission have done more, much more towards the prosperity of it thus far, than the men. . . . I will further add that could any female know before she left her home, all the trials and afflictions through which she must inevitably pass, she would not of herself have strength or grace to enlist in so great an enterprize. I think I may say the same of man.

The missionaries sailed, and soon afterward, reluctantly leaving his wife and infant daughter in New England, Morse traveled to Washington, D.C., via New York City, to paint President Monroe at the White House. Arriving in early December, 1819, he was kindly received and given a painting room, but he was frustrated by the president's crowded schedule, once waiting all day for a ten-minute sitting. Still, he worked quickly and successfully, writing on December 17: "I have succeeded to my satisfaction, and, what is better, to the satisfaction of himself and family; so much so that one of his daughters wishes me to copy the head for her.

*The elder Bromfield (1727–1820), fa-
ther of Jedidiah Morse's London agent,
had been in the family's British-American
merchant trade. As the Revolution
neared, "the consequent embarrassments
in mercantile affairs" had induced Henry
Bromfield "to seek rural retirement" in
Harvard, Massachusetts, in 1765. He
lived fifty-five years there, thirty-five of
them alone after his wife died. In 1813 he
wrote, "I have to fear a solitary winter.... The fireside is most consonant to my
age and my feelings."*

They all say that mine is the best that has been taken of him. The daughter told me (she said as a secret) that her father was delighted with it, and said it was the only one that in his opinion looked like him; and this, too, with Stuart's in the room."

Of course this head would have been on an average-size canvas, not the large canvas that would be used for the full-length Charleston commission. Morse carried this back to Charleston with him at the end of December, and from it produced the large formal portrait. The painting was not completed until the following year, 1820, in Boston. Unhappily, the full-length Monroe suffers in comparison. Morse found it difficult to contrive the pose and composition. Even the head became more stilted and, oddly, less dignified. Though he borrowed from Stuart's "Lansdowne" portrait of Washington, it is clear that Morse's genius was hampered by the absence of a sitter, of the tangible, visible fact of a face, which he had always been so successful at capturing.

Reverend and Mrs. Hiram Bingham

1819. Oil on millboard, 10 x 8″
Yale University Art Gallery,
New Haven, Connecticut
Gift of Hiram Bingham, B.A., 1898

Bingham (1789–1869) and his wife, born Sybil Moseley (d. 1848), were missionaries in Honolulu for twenty years. He translated part of the Bible into the Hawaiian language and wrote many hymns, which he often accompanied on the cello he had brought with him. His influence among the chiefs led to strict laws governing morality, which not surprisingly were greatly resented by American seamen in port, who twice physically assaulted him.

The painting was meant to hang in City Hall as a pendant to John Trumbull's *George Washington* (as it still does). Morse created an effective contrast between the two: interior versus exterior, intellect versus action, Federalist versus revolutionary. But in this first implicit confrontation between two artists whose mutual antipathy was to ripen, Trumbull, it must be said, won the round.

The 1820 season began auspiciously. "I am doing well, although the city fairly swarms with painters. I am the only one that has as much as he can do; all the rest are complaining." The exhibition of his full-length portrait of Sally Alston brought him much praise.

Morse's Charleston clients came from the whole spectrum of its (enfranchised) society. They were not only planters like Colonel Alston but doctors, lawyers, clergymen, and, in the case of Alexander Calder, a cabinetmaker and builder. In Morse's fine portrait, Calder is a confident, upright, unaffected Scotsman. His ruddy-skinned, heavy-lidded face shines out atop a powerful torso clad in a dark green jacket and crisp white stock and collar. The rather arbitrary bold red swatch of drapery at the right makes an effective counterpoint to the dark jacket, while the aquamarine sky touched with rose lends a quiet note of approaching evening.

According to the Charleston *Courier* of November 10, 1819, Calder had just returned to town after "having retired for a time on business to Europe"; it is likely that he had been absent all that year until then. Morse did not return to Charleston for his third season until January, 1820, the year I believe the portrait to have been painted. The commission was probably occasioned by Calder's initiation in 1819 into the St. Andrew's Society of Charleston, the fraternal and charitable society then celebrating its ninetieth year. The previous spring the society's hall had served as residence for President Monroe. With this recognition Calder had arrived socially, and the portrait by Morse would have confirmed his status.

The companion portraits of Robert Young Hayne and his wife are unhappily no longer together, except in these pages. Although he never attended college, Hayne was admitted to the bar at the age of twenty and at various times served in the state legislature, the U.S. Senate, and as governor of South Carolina. In 1820, when this portrait was probably painted, he was the attorney general of the state. Morse and Hayne were the same age and, moreover, cousins by marriage. The late Dr. Finley's wife, Mary Peronneau, had been Mrs. Robert Young in her first marriage, and Hayne's aunt, to whom he was devoted. He had promised the dying Dr. Finley that he would be like a son to her. Although Morse and Hayne were probably already acquainted, the depressing circumstances would have brought them closer together.

Hayne's portrait is the very picture of youthful success—a candid, confident, intelligent face, enhanced by the simplicity of the setting and attitude and the sobriety of color. The warm-toned skin, auburn hair, and patch of red upholstery, however, harmonize with the hotter pinks and reds of his wife's portrait. The brilliant rendering of the textures and transparencies of fabrics that Morse had developed during his previous Charleston sojourns makes the painting of Mrs. Hayne a stunning tour de force. Together with the elegance of the pose and the smooth, homogeneous surface, it also suggests that the influence of Thomas Sully had superseded that of Gilbert Stuart.

It is believed that Morse had visited Sully in Philadelphia in November, 1819, on his way to Washington. If so, he probably saw Sully's recently completed portrait of Andrew Jackson then on exhibition at the Association of American Artists on Chestnut Street. The cursive brushwork of that painting may well have influenced Morse's handling of the heads of James Monroe and Robert Hayne. His brush is equally supple in Mrs. Hayne's portrait, but it is his striking palette that suggests he has taken a page from Sully. Nonetheless, there is a special accentuation of the vivid colors that is distinctively Morse's. Increasingly bold or uncommon colors in unusual combinations mark many of his paintings from this time on.

Sully's influence, while significant, is always modified by Morse's own creative realism. Even when he permits himself romantic inflections, his vision is grounded in material reality. In this, he is part of a definably American mode of painting, in which the artist relies on his imaginative eye to record faithfully his sitter's face and form, trusting that record to reveal his or her life history—that which is commonly called character. It also explains Morse's relative lack of success in the realm of history painting, where imaginative invention is requisite.

The agrarian economy of Charleston was entering a recession. Bank failures following the panic of 1819 had crippled the cotton growers because of their dependence on New York banks for the financing to transport their crop to market. Charleston art patronage began to dry up, and this, combined with Morse's loneliness, made him think increasingly of abandoning the South.

Morse returned to his family, now in New Haven, in the spring. In August he wrote to the younger Henry Bromfield in England: "You will perceive by the heading of this letter that I am in New Haven. My father and his family have left Charlestown, Massachusetts, and are settled in this place. My own family also, consisting of wife and daughter, are pleasantly settled in this delightful spot. I have built me a fine painting-room attached to my house in which I paint my large pictures in the summer, and in the winter I migrate to Charleston, South Carolina, where I have commissions sufficient to employ me for some years to come." The last sentence expresses an optimism he no longer felt. Charleston was losing its appeal.

A portrait of Morse's wife, resplendent in a richly colored dress, has been placed as early as 1819 and as late as 1822. Although its style and Lucretia's costume suggest the South Carolina portraits, her apparent age and a greater fleshiness than seen in the 1818 chalk portrait suggest that it may have been done in the summer of 1820.

He returned to the South for his last season in the autumn, remaining until early April, 1821. Just after Christmas he wrote to Lucretia, who was pregnant with their second child. "I feel the separation this time more than ever, and I felt the other day, when I saw the steamship start for New York, that I had almost a mind to return in her." He had taken with him the full-length portrait of President Monroe and another of Mrs. Caroline Ball, which he had finished in New

Dr. and Mrs. Thomas Holman

1819. Oil on millboard, 10 x 8"
Yale University Art Gallery,
New Haven, Connecticut
Gift of Harrison F. Bassett

Dr. Holman (1793–1826) and his wife, Lucia Ruggles (1793–1886), were married on September 26 before sailing with the Binghams on the Thaddeus *on October 23, 1819. Their portrait is more genial and colorful, as befits a wedding portrait. The strong modeling of his face and the energetic design of her collar emphasize his intelligence and her independent nature. Mrs. Holman's brother, Samuel Ruggles, and his wife were also in the ship's company.*

Mrs. Robert Young Hayne

c. 1820. Oil on canvas, 30¼ x 25⅛"
The Chrysler Museum, Norfolk, Virginia, Gift of
Mrs. William Sloane in memory of Margaret Bell
Irvine, The Norfolk Society of Arts, and Museum
Membership Purchase by Exchange

*After the death of his first wife, a daughter
of Charles Cotesworth Pinckney, Hayne
married a daughter of Colonel William
Alston. Rebecca Motte Alston, the subject
of this portrait, was "of more than ordinary strength of character and intelligence." As the wedding was probably early
in 1820, these portraits may commemo-
rate the event.*

Haven. That of Mrs. Ball (now lost) had been praised by John Trumbull and
John Vanderlyn and was also admired in Charleston, but apparently not by the
sitter.

"Mrs. Ball wants some alterations, that is to say every five minutes she would
like to be different. . . . Derangement is her only apology." Then she refused to
pay him the agreed fee, withholding four hundred dollars, bitterly conceding
that she could not afford to pay and blaming it on crop failure. This brought out
the caustic streak in Morse's nature that would reappear in later life in his polemical pamphlets. "Madam," his letter to her began, "Supposing that I was dealing
not only with a woman of honor, but, from her professions, with a Christian, I
ventured . . . to make an appeal to your conscience. . . . Must I understand . . .
that the goodness or badness of your crop is the scale on which your conscience
measures your obligation to pay a just debt?"

Robert Young Hayne

c. 1820. Oil on canvas, 30 x 25″
State of South Carolina
Governor's Mansion, Columbia

In the U.S. Senate from 1822 to 1832, Hayne (1791–1839) rapidly became a brilliant proponent of states' rights and nullification, culminating in a famous 1830 debate with Daniel Webster. For two weeks the pair attracted throngs ·to listen to the "cadenced flow" of choice oratory. Senator Thomas Hart Benton described this amiable, expressive face as "the reflex of his head and his heart and ready for the artist who could seize the moment to paint to the life."

But there was to be one final significant commission before Morse quit Charleston. It was a portrait of the Reverend Nathaniel Bowen, since 1818 rector of Saint Michael's Church and Episcopal bishop of South Carolina. Among Morse's half-length portraits, it is the most complex composition since that of Colonel Drayton. The inventive pose shows the bishop standing at his lectern, his left hand turning the pages of the Scriptures, his head turned to his right. A Gothic pier and doorway are seen behind him, while a red curtain falls in folds and clusters to his right shoulder. The textures of his clerical robes are vividly rendered, but perhaps the most effective aspect of the portrait is the lighting, which both unifies and dramatizes the picture. Especially striking is the light playing over the hand on the Bible, creating a trompe-l'oeil immediacy while suggesting a symbolic radiance.

Even while patronage in Charleston declined, an Academy of Arts was

Lucretia Pickering Walker Morse

c.1820. Oil on canvas, 30 x 25″
Mead Art Museum, Amherst College,
Massachusetts
Bequest of Herbert L. Pratt, '95

While living in Charleston, Lucretia al-
ways dressed well. Samuel's ever-sober
brother Richard, then living in Savan-
nah, disapproved of her ostentation.
Nonetheless, as Samuel pointed out, all
her dresses had been made "in Boston un-
der Mama's superintendence." The elder
Mrs. Morse had enjoyed "lace and puffed
skirts" when younger; with no surviving
daughters, she must have relished seeing
her daughter-in-law handsomely clad.
Though this portrait was probably painted
in New Haven, the splendid dress seems
reminiscent of the luxurious tastes of the
southern city.

Reverend Nathaniel Bowen

1821. Oil on canvas, 36 x 29″
Grace Church, New York

Bowen (1779–1839) was born in Boston
of a clerical family. Reared in Charleston,
South Carolina, he returned to New En-
gland, where he studied theology and was
admitted to the Episcopal priesthood.
From 1802 to 1809 he served Saint Mi-
chael's Church in Charleston while reor-
ganizing the Diocese of South Carolina.
His move to Grace Church in New York
was in part born of financial necessity, but
the ill health of his wife and other circum-
stances necessitated his taking winter
leaves of absence in the South. He re-
turned there as bishop for the last twenty
years of his life.

founded in 1821 to encourage it. Morse was one of the directors and, with the ex-ample of the Royal Academy behind him, was asked to draft rules for the new or-ganization. Although he strongly favored its establishment, he must have recognized how bad the timing was. "I feel not very sanguine as to its success." (It expired in 1830.) Very soon he made up his mind to abandon Charleston for good. On March 31 he wrote to let Lucretia know that "your husband will be with you as soon, if not sooner, than this letter." He did not know that on March 12 their second daughter had been born and, within a few days, had died.

I MIGRATE TO CHARLESTON

Reverend Nathaniel Bowen

V. "The National Hall"

W HEN MORSE RETURNED TO NEW HAVEN from the South, a new phase in his art began. Quite soon he produced a painting that, after his death, became his best-known work. Despite his great success as a fashionable portraitist in Charleston, he had not lost his desire to introduce the "great style" of history painting to America. To that end he conceived the idea of painting large canvases of the representatives of the federal government: the members of the House and the Senate in their respective chambers in the Capitol and the president and his Cabinet in the White House drawing room.

It was natural that he should think of Washington as a source of subject matter and patronage. His contacts in the capital were impeccable. President Monroe was an admirer of his work; former Senator James Hillhouse was a next-door neighbor in New Haven and Congressman Joel R. Poinsett a friend from South Carolina; and his father was at that time preparing a report on the condition of the eastern Indian tribes at the behest of Secretary of State John C. Calhoun.

America was aglow with nationalistic pride in the decade following the conclusion of the War of 1812. One result was the willingness of Congress in 1817 to commission four large paintings from John Trumbull for the newly completed Rotunda of the Capitol. When he had finished the first of these, *The Declaration of Independence*, he exhibited it first in New York at his American Academy of the Fine Arts and then sent it on a highly profitable tour of Boston, Hartford, and Baltimore before presenting it to Congress in early 1819.

It was the high point of Trumbull's career, and Morse must have taken heart from his success. Not only had a history painting proved popular with the American public, but it was a history painting in accord with Morse's own convictions. Static, symbolic, a documentary rather than a dramatic painting, it appealed to the moral sense and to the ideal of democracy. Furthermore, Trumbull accomplished this goal through portraits of the men who had brought forth the ideal. It must, in most respects, have provided the inspiration for Morse's painting *The House of Representatives*, begun in late 1821.

Between his return to New Haven in April and his departure for Washington in November, Morse renewed his friendship and studies with his former professor Benjamin Silliman, accompanying him on a geology expedition in the

68

JOHN TRUMBULL (1756–1843)
The Declaration of Independence

1819. Oil on canvas, 144 x 216″
United States Capitol Art Collection,
Washington, D.C.

*The importance of this painting for
Morse's* House of Representatives *lies
in Trumbull's decision to present the
"wonderful moment when tension and
conflict have been resolved and an idea
has triumphed" (Irma B. Jaffe,* John
Trumbull: Five Paintings of the Revolution, *Wadsworth Atheneum, Hartford, Connecticut, 1975).*

Berkshires and catching up on developments in the science of electricity, to
which he had been introduced at Yale. He also thought of establishing an academy of art in New Haven, modeled after the one just founded in Charleston, and
he even composed a series of lectures, but nothing came of it. He made designs
for a marble-carving machine to facilitate the replication of sculpture, only to discover two years later that someone had secured a patent before him.

When he arrived in Washington, he wasted no time. He was given studio
space just off the floor of the House of Representatives, newly rebuilt after the
British burning of the Capitol. (Superseded by the present hall in 1857, it is now
known as Statuary Hall.) First he turned his attention to the hall itself. One of the
grandest rooms in America (though less magnificent than before the fire), it had
been rebuilt according to Benjamin Latrobe's plans by his successor, Charles
Bulfinch. Congress first met in the new hall in December, 1819. Fully aware of its
grandeur, and even more so of its democratic significance, Morse made the hall
itself the symbolic focus of his painting.

The immense half dome (then illusionistically painted with simulated cof-
fers) made a perspective rendering of the space difficult. Three times he drew it
and three times erased it. With the help of a camera obscura he finally solved the
problem to his satisfaction. On February 16, 1822 (when only the architectural
setting was on the canvas), a writer for the *National Intelligencer* loftily pronounced it "mathematically correct." More to the point, no interior scene of such
monumentality had ever been painted in America. Morse's most telling decision
was to present the House in night session, illuminated by the Argand oil lamps of
the great chandelier. The resonant, almost reverent, glow of light lends its own
symbolic power and evokes the pervasive quietude and suspension of time that
characterize the picture.

Morse's difficulties with the perspective rendering of the House chamber are clear from this study. An important part of his solution was to include more of the colonnade and the doorway, so that the cornice wraps around to the picture surface. Thus to the rigidly perspectival view of the camera obscura he added an accumulation of views made possible by the moving eye, achieving a grander vista.

This is probably the first of fifteen or sixteen versions of the immensely popular painting. Three are reported to be in Capuchin churches in New York City and Yonkers, perhaps accounting for the many copies by American artists.

Beginning with Dunlap, it has often been said that in this setting Morse was decisively influenced by François-Marius Granet's *Choir of the Capuchin Church in Rome*, painted in Rome in 1815. Much replicated by the artist, it also inspired numerous copies in America. One by Thomas Sully was exhibited with great success. The dominance of the vaulted interior and the magical atmosphere of reflected lights and half shadows surely contributed to Morse's inspiration. There are significant differences between Granet's painting and Morse's, including the subject matter and the perspective arrangement. Granet's traditional box structure was undoubtedly much easier to render than Morse's complex interior.

With the architectural setting achieved, Morse began the task of painting the small-scale likenesses of the men who would inhabit it. The proximity of Morse's painting room to the House floor permitted his sitters to come to him at their convenience and return to the floor when the call bell indicated a vote or they were otherwise needed on short notice. Some of his sitters asked him to paint a second portrait for themselves, for which they paid twenty dollars. Morse worked rapidly on the study heads. He took the first likenesses on January 2, 1822, and by the end of the month his father, in Washington to present his Indian report, wrote that Samuel had completed sixty-three heads. In mid-February he returned home to New Haven with more than eighty heads and his large canvas ready to receive them.

From the evidence of two that have been definitely identified, these were done on small millboard panels (less than six inches high) and were only of the head or head and shoulders. Moreover, and this is especially interesting, they were painted in the attitude *and* the lighting in which they would appear in the final painting. Thus, though none is known to survive, Morse must have prepared a drawing or oil study in which the congressmen and others were assigned their exact positions in the hall. It is clear that he gave careful thought not only to the compositional configuration of groups but also to the placement of individuals.

Key to *The House of Representatives*

Morse's own key identified eighty-six figures, incompletely and sometimes inaccurately. The amplified list given here attempts to clarify the identity of those depicted. Since the interpretation of the painting involves both the Sixteenth (March 4, 1819, to March 3, 1821) and Seventeenth (March 4, 1821, to March 3, 1823) Congress, we have indicated a member's service in one or both.

1. Joseph Gales, reporter
2. William W. Seaton, reporter
3. Thomas Dunn, of Maryland, Sergeant at Arms (16th/17th)
4. O. Dunn, Assistant Doorkeeper
5. Lewis Williams, North Carolina (16th/17th)
6. Josiah Crudup, North Carolina (17th)
7. William Hendricks, Indiana (16th/17th)
8. Anthony New, Kentucky (17th)
9. John Cocke, Tennessee (16th/17th)
10. Philip P. Barbour, Virginia (16th; Speaker, 17th)
11. Thomas Dougherty, Clerk of the House (16th/17th; d.1822)
12. Samuel Smith, Maryland (16th/17th)
13. William Eustis, Massachusetts (16th/17th)
14. Daniel P. Cook, Illinois (16th/17th)
15. Ebenezer Stoddard, Connecticut (17th)
16. ex-Senator James Hillhouse, Connecticut (resigned 1810)
17. ex-Senator David Daggett, Connecticut (till 1819)
18. Solomon Van Rensselaer, New York (16th/17th)

19. Littleton W. Tazewell, a commissioner of claims under the 1819 Treaty with Spain (ratified 1821)
20. Thomas Newton, Jr., Virginia (16th/17th)
21. Justice Thomas Todd
22. Justice Gabriel Duval
23. John W. Campbell, Ohio (16th/17th)
24. Samuel Eddy, Rhode Island (16th/17th)
25. Hugh Nelson, Virginia (16th/17th)
26. Justice Bushrod Washington
27. Justice Henry Brockholst Livingston
28. Chief Justice John Marshall
29. Justice Joseph Story
30. Lewis Bigelow, Massachusetts (17th)
31. Timothy Fuller, Massachusetts (16th/17th)
32. John Scott, Missouri (took his seat December 3, 1821)
33. John Rhea, Tennessee (16th/17th)
34. John W. Taylor, New York (16th/17th; second Speaker, 16th, from November 15, 1820, succeeding Henry Clay)
35. Joseph Hemphill, Pennsylvania (16th/17th)
36. Edward F. Tatnall, Georgia (17th)
37. Noyes Barber, Connecticut (17th)
38. John Randolph, Virginia (16th/17th)
39. Gabriel Moore, Alabama (17th)
40. Walter Patterson, New York (17th)
41. Richard McCarty, New York (17th)
42. Charles Hooks, North Carolina (16th/17th)
43. Mark L. Hill, Massachusetts (16th) and Maine (17th)
44. John D. Dickinson, New York (16th/17th)

45. George McDuffie, South Carolina (17th)
46. James Blair, South Carolina (17th)
47. Henry W. Dwight, Massachusetts (17th)
48. Joel R. Poinsett, South Carolina (17th)
49. Henry R. Warfield, Maryland (16th/17th)
50. John Russ, Connecticut (16th/17th)
51. Josiah S. Johnston, Louisiana (17th)
52. Churchill C. Cambreleng, New York (17th)
53. Christopher Rankin, Mississippi (16th/17th)
54. Robert Allen, Tennessee (16th/17th)
55. [Arthur, or William?] Smith, Virginia (17th)
56. Jonathan Russell, Massachusetts (17th)
57. Gideon Tomlinson, Connecticut (16th/17th)
58. Elias Keyes, Vermont (17th)
59. Louis McLane, Delaware (16th/17th)
60. William S. Blackledge, North Carolina (16th/17th)
61. Cadwallader D. Colden (17th)
62. William Lowndes, South Carolina (16th/17th)
63. Charles F. Mercer, Virginia (16th/17th)
64. James McSherry, Pennsylvania (17th)
65. William Milnor, Pennsylvania (17th)
66. Joshua Cushman, Massachusetts (16th) and Maine (17th)

67. Alexander Smyth, Virginia (16th/17th)
68. John Findlay, Pennsylvania (17th)
69. Aaron Hobart, Massachusetts (16th/17th)
70. John Sergeant, Pennsylvania (16th/17th)
71. Albert H. Tracy, New York (16th/17th)
72. Thomas Whipple, Jr., New Hampshire (17th)
73. Enoch Lincoln, Massachusetts (16th) and Maine (17th)
74. William Plumer, Jr., New Hampshire (16th/17th)
75. Henry Baldwin, Pennsylvania (16th/17th)
76. J. Dunn, Servant
77. Andrew Stewart, Pennsylvania (17th)
78. Nathaniel Upham, New Hampshire (16th/17th)
79. Benjamin Birch, of Maryland, Doorkeeper (17th)
80. William D. Williamson, Maine (17th)
81. Henry W. Edwards, Connecticut (16th/17th)
82. Jedidiah Morse
83. Benjamin Silliman
84. Petalesharro, a Pawnee chief
85. Rollin C. Mallary, Vermont (16th/17th)
86. C. Dunn, Servant

Joseph Gales

This study for the figure at the extreme left of The House of Representatives *is revealing of Morse's method. Gales is painted in the same size, lighting, and attitude in which he appears in the large painting. An initial, detailed compositional study with figures must have existed. Gales (1786–1860) came to America as a child with his parents, political refugees from England. Well educated, he learned the trades of printer and reporter and in 1807 joined the staff of the* National Intelligencer, *which reported congressional proceedings. By 1810 he was sole proprietor and from 1812 ran the paper in partnership with William W. Seaton, his brother-in-law (standing beside him in Morse's large picture). Until 1833 their reports were the primary record of congressional debates. Gales and Seaton also published the* Annals of Congress *and the* American State Papers, *which covered the years up to 1861. Both served as mayor of the City of Washington.*

In New Haven he began the long process of integrating his figures into his architecture, which monopolized his time for the remainder of 1822. After a brief local showing, the painting was sent to Boston, where Morse made some changes suggested by Washington Allston. Although the advertisement for the Boston exhibition of his picture in February, 1823, announced that it contained eighty-eight portraits, there are in fact ninety-four figures, of whom eighty-six are identified in Morse's key.

This key and an accompanying description sold for twelve and a half cents over the twenty-five-cent admission fee. (A nice marketing touch was the offer of "season tickets" for only fifty cents.) Almost all of the thousand-word description was devoted to the architecture and its decoration, including measurements and materials. Morse was explicit about this emphasis: "The primary design of the present picture is not so much to give a highly finished likeness of the individuals introduced, as to exhibit to the public a faithful representation of the National Hall, with its furniture and business during the session of Congress. If the individuals are simply recognized by their acquaintance as likenesses, the whole design of the painter will be answered." Despite these prosaic words, Morse surely infused far greater meaning into this grand scene than he chose to articulate, as the character and composition of the painting itself bear witness.

The eighty-six men named by Morse included sixty-eight congressmen, the six justices of the Supreme Court, the commissioner of the 1819 treaty with Spain (the Florida purchase), the two editors of the *National Intelligencer*, one sergeant-at-arms, one clerk, two doorkeepers, and two young servants. All of them are depicted on the floor of the House. There are three identified figures in the balcony: from the right, the Pawnee chief Petalesharro, Benjamin Silliman, and Jedidiah Morse. The fourth figure is unidentified, as are seven on the House floor, including the prominently silhouetted lamplighter.

Morse grouped his figures cogently. The congressmen are disposed in seemingly random but coherent small groups. The placement of some individuals is surely significant; for example, Philip P. Barbour of Virginia was Speaker of the House for the Seventeenth Congress (1821–23) and is therefore placed in front of the Speaker's desk, the tenth figure from the left.

More pointedly, the justices, together with several legislators and the commissioner, are grouped on a raised platform behind a red-draped railing at the back left, together with an elaborately framed engraved copy of the Declaration of Independence. (It should be noted that the two men in conversation at the left of this group are not members of the House but former senators. James Hillhouse and David Daggett of Connecticut were New Haven neighbors of Morse, who granted them honorary inclusion.) Four of the justices are to the right of the Declaration (Chief Justice John Marshall is second from the right), while two are to the left. An open aisle at the left further draws our attention to them.

The Supreme Court was then located inside the Capitol, and the House was then the only popularly elected legislative body. The special emphasis on the closely aligned justices—representing the principle of constitutional law, flanking the Declaration of Independence, and surveying the diverse group of the

THE NATIONAL HALL

people's representatives with their conflicting desires and demands—is surely not merely fortuitous. Although Morse does not articulate any symbolic intention in his letters or in his description, he certainly does so in his painting.

In the six years preceding his work in the Capitol, six states had entered the Union—three southern, three northern—and the most recent was Missouri (August 10, 1821), admitted as a slave state. When Morse arrived in Washington, the outrage and bitterness of the debates between northern and southern states that preceded the Missouri Compromise (there were now twelve free and twelve slave states) had only just subsided.

A key figure in the compromise was Representative Mark Langdon Hill of Massachusetts (District of Maine). In Morse's picture, Hill is standing in the center foreground, handsomely cloaked, his face glowing in the warm half-light. Larger than the other congressmen, he is in many respects the dominant figure among them. When Henry Clay succeeded in tying the admission of Maine as a separate state to the admission of Missouri, many people in Maine were aghast. It was Hill who was instrumental in arranging the Senate-House conference that separated the bills. In return, Hill and John Holmes, alone among the Maine District delegates, voted for the admission of Missouri under the famous compromise terms. Without their votes the provision would have failed. The two men were vilified by their opponents, but no less an authority than James Madison wrote to commend Hill: "The candid view you have given of the Missouri question is well calculated to assuage the party zeal which it generated. As long as the conciliatory spirit which produced the Constitution remains in the mass of people, and the several parts of the Union understand the deep interest, which every other part has in maintaining it, these stormy subjects will soon blow over."

Though it was to prove delusive, the restored unanimity of the Congress and the country is solemnly and consciously embodied in the muted glow and unifying space of this dignified painting.

As the Missouri Compromise had been the major achievement of the Sixteenth Congress, so Indian policy was the preoccupation of the Seventeenth. As previously noted, Secretary of State Calhoun had commissioned Jedidiah Morse (February 7, 1820) to explore the conditions of the Indian tribes east of the Mississippi and prepare a report on his findings and recommendations. In the summer of 1820 he had traveled more than two thousand miles, by steamboat and canoe, as far as Green Bay, in the Northwest Territory, and for a year thereafter he labored on his written account. This extraordinary effort on the part of a sixty-year-old pastor of uncertain health and precarious finances resulted in a message that was, for its day, remarkably sensitive to the plight of the Indians—a sentiment shared by the Monroe administration—although, naturally, the report's ultimate aim was their conversion and salvation through Calvinist Christianity. It was presented to Congress in January, 1822, while Samuel was busily recording the features of the members. The idealism of Jedidiah's report, like the idealism of his son's painting, went mostly unheeded.

The inclusion of Jedidiah and a Pawnee Indian in the gallery of the House suggests that the evening session about to convene was to discuss the Morse re-

William D. Williamson

1822. Oil on millboard, 5 x 3½"
Mattatuck Museum of the Mattatuck Historical
Society, Waterbury, Connecticut

Charles Walker Morse gave this sketch to a friend in 1883, saying that it was "for his [father's] large painting of the U.S. Senate [sic]." It was later misidentified as a portrait of Cyrus West Field, who was three years old in 1822! William D. Williamson (1779–1846) of Maine, who served only in the Seventeenth Congress, is the last seated congressman at the right, seen in conversation with Henry W. Edwards of Connecticut, who leans on the partition. Williamson is known primarily for his History of the State of Maine.

port. The Pawnee, Petalesharro, was in Washington with an Indian delegation meeting with the president and other federal officials. An episode of moral valor, in which Petalesharro had saved a woman of another tribe from death by fire at the hands of his own people, had been published by the editors of the *National Intelligencer* (seen at the extreme left of Morse's painting) at the end of January. In an early example of instant media fame, Petalesharro was lionized in Washington, and his portrait was painted by Charles Bird King. So impressed was the Reverend Morse with the edifying tale of Indian morality that he retold it in his report and commissioned an engraving of the portrait for the frontispiece.

Samuel Morse's idealistic, intellectual painting thus construed becomes at once a reminder of contemporary events of the utmost significance, an apotheosis of democratic government, and a proud personal tribute to his father. It is far from the clamorous, discordant, contentious reality of the House of Representatives whose "vulgar demeanor" so astonished de Tocqueville. Morse knew this, of course, and it was surely a mistake not to tell the public in so many words that he offered them a glorious ideal, not a prosaic reality. Instead of an inventory of architectural and decorative detail, a catalogue of democratic virtues would have alerted his audience to the theme they never perceived. His subject is the heroism of an idea, to which he bears witness but which he does not dramatize.

Unlike the famous John Trumbull, Morse was a young painter whose reputation as a portraitist had only recently been established. He could not expect Congress to commission this painting; indeed, it had taken Trumbull decades to win his Rotunda commissions. Asking only the cooperation of Congress, Morse undertook his task on speculation, in the fond belief that he could not fail to earn a substantial income from the public exhibition of the painting, as Trumbull and others had done. Although it is often assumed that he hoped Congress would purchase the work, there is no evidence for this. Certainly he hoped that its success would recommend him to Congress for other federal commissions, such as the remaining four spaces in the Rotunda. In this hope he was to be disappointed, and so began an intermittent, often bitter, campaign by Morse and his supporters that would span twenty-five years.

The Boston exhibition of his most ambitious painting, at Doggett's Repository on Market Street, began well enough, but attendance soon dropped away. Morse closed the show on April 12, 1823, after a run of about seven weeks. Allston wrote a letter of condolence and support, suggesting that New York would offer a less apathetic response and assuring Morse that the picture "has yet gained you a full harvest of praise.... There is but one opinion concerning it— that it does you great honour.... Besides, its career is but *just begun*."

Another career just begun was that of Charles Walker Morse, born to Lucretia and Samuel on March 17, 1823. The joy of the event was tempered by the increased pressure on Morse to earn a living sufficient to move his growing family out of his parents' crowded home and support them independently. He placed great hopes on the New York exhibition of this work, but there he encountered competition from other exhibition pictures, notably Rembrandt Peale's mam-

Detail from *The House of Representatives*

This section from the center of the painting includes Mark L. Hill of Maine in the foreground, John Scott of Missouri and the white-maned John Rhea of Tennessee in the left middle ground, and, just behind the latter, John W. Taylor of New York, who had succeeded Henry Clay as Speaker of the House during the Sixteenth Congress. Thus three men instrumental in or symbolic of the Missouri Compromise are grouped in the center of the painting beneath the immense, glowing chandelier.

moth and melancholy *Court of Death*, which earned its author great sums. Once again, it was only seven weeks before Morse withdrew *The House of Representatives* from exhibition on July 16. Henry Pratt, who managed the tour of the painting, noted that New Yorkers were sated with amusements, "and I believe it to be a fact that exhibitions are so multiplied that people begin to think them not worth seeing."

The eccentric poet and geologist James Gates Percival, whose portrait Morse painted that same year, wrote about the debacle to a friend:

I will tell you one thing sub rosa. *Morse's picture of Congress Hall, (have you seen it? if not it is too late now,) that picture has cost him one hundred and ten dollars to exhibit it in New*

The House of Representatives

1821–23 (dated 1822). Oil on canvas,
86½ x 130¾"
The Corcoran Gallery of Art, Washington, D.C.

After its unsuccessful tour, Morse put the painting in storage. Although William Dunlap wrote that it was sold to an unidentified gentleman—"and our House of Representatives in a body [was] removed to Great Britain"—in fact Morse himself must have sent the painting to England, where Charles Robert Leslie tried to find a buyer for it. In 1829 it was sold to Sherman Converse for one thousand dollars and exhibited in London. In December, 1847, Morse received a letter from the artist Francis W. Edmonds, who wrote that he had seen the painting, "which has been sent to [New York] from London.... We found it at the store of Coates & Co., No. 54 Exchange place, nailed against a board partition in the third story, almost invisible from the dirt and dust upon it.... Having no strainer, its surface is as uneven as the waves of the sea.... Excuse me for troubling you in this matter, but, believing it to be one of the best works ever painted by you... I could not patiently be silent while [it is] in its present condition." Edmonds was startled by Morse's reply, in which he disowned his paintings: "they must take their chances in the world—he cared no further about them." It was left to Morse's student Daniel Huntington to rescue the picture, and it was from Huntington's estate that the Corcoran purchased it in 1911.

Alexander Metcalf Fisher

Reverend Jeremiah Day

1823. Oil on canvas, 50 x 40"
Yale University Art Gallery,
New Haven, Connecticut
Gift of the Class of 1823

A large canvas allowed Morse to place the tall, spare figure of Day within a resonant space, subtly but firmly constructed. Using much higher color than usual in the face, hands, chair back, and tablecloth, the artist also painted a splendid contrast in the glowing black coat.

York. Tell it not in Gath! He labored at it eighteen months, and spent many hundred dollars in its execution; and now he has to pay the public for looking at it, 'largess, largess'. . . . Who would write or paint any good thing for such a fashionable vulgar *as ours? . . . If some sign-painter had only painted Nettleton preaching up an awakening, and sent it about the country, he would have filled his pockets with it, and so would Morse too.*

Although the painting was sent on to Albany, Hartford, and Middletown, it continued to lose money. Morse put it in storage and went out looking for portraits to paint.

During the intensive work on *The House of Representatives* in 1822, there had been little time for other commissions. An exception was the posthumous portrait of Alexander Metcalf Fisher, a Yale professor who had perished in a shipwreck off the coast of Ireland on April 22 of that year, age only twenty-seven,

Alexander Metcalf Fisher

1822. Oil on canvas, 44⅛ x 34¾"
Yale University Art Gallery,
New Haven, Connecticut
Gift of Professor Fisher's Colleagues in Office, 1822

Although Morse may have known Fisher (1794–1822), he used a portrait by Lucius Munson as model for the features. The elaborate, detailed setting was occasioned by the commemorative purpose of the painting.

James Gates Percival

while sailing to France for study and recuperation. The elegant, sumptuously painted image conveys both acuity and frailty, the slender body enveloped in heavy clothing, broadly disposed. Just as a book is often the symbol of fame, so the blank pages on which Fisher is about to write signify his unfulfilled promise.

Fisher had succeeded the Reverend Jeremiah Day as professor of mathematics and natural philosophy when the latter succeeded Timothy Dwight as president of the college. Possibly as a result of the success of his portrait of Fisher, Morse was commissioned by the Class of 1823 to paint that of the Reverend Jeremiah Day. President Day's intellectual sphere is indicated by the two closed tomes, *Tenets of Philosophy* and *Algebra*, and by the open book and compass, which allude to the treatise he was then writing on "conic sections, spherical geography and trigonometry." The linking of mathematics and philosophy was especially common in the eighteenth century, when Descartes had applied the clear, deductive method of the former to the latter and from such logical proceedings "proved" the existence of himself and of God. Jeremiah Day was heir to the Cartesian system.

James Gates Percival, whose remarks on Morse's New York exhibition have been quoted, was no Cartesian. Instead of the mathematician-philosopher's lucid world, Percival sought the "Poet's World," where "other suns, /And other stars" would light

> a spiritual flame
> Warming and kindling into higher life
> Our perishable frames, here poor and weak,
> The creatures of decay. . . .

When Percival died he was serving as state geologist of Wisconsin, and a contemporary remembered him as an "undemonstrative, noiseless, passionless man . . . a creature of pure intellect," but his poetry, his letters, and above all his appearance as seized by Morse in a small portrait of him, probably in May, 1823, reveal quite another aspect.

Whimsical, reclusive, sickly, he was a compulsive reader from childhood and intensely interested in nearly every subject he encountered. Although he graduated from Yale Medical School with distinction, he scarcely practiced. Poetry and geology were his great passions. He translated the *Prometheus* of Aeschylus into verse in six days, and also translated from Russian, Serbian, Hungarian, and many other languages. Considered the leading American poet before Bryant's rise, he published some five volumes of poetry, which is seldom read today. In addition, he edited Webster's Dictionary, in which, he said, "I took more pleasure . . . than in anything else I have done."

On March 30, 1823, one of New Haven's nonacademic figures wrote to Morse:

> *Mr. D. C. DeForest's compliments to Mr. Morse. Mr. DeForest desires to have his portrait taken such as it would have been six or eight years ago, making the necessary calculation for it, and at the same time making it a good likeness in all other respects.*

David Curtis DeForest

1823. Oil on canvas, 34¼ x 25¼"
Museo Nacional de Bellas Artes,
Buenos Aires Argentina

This perceptively characterized portrait was at one time attributed to Francisco Goya. The mistake is not as surprising as it may seem when one compares the work to some of Goya's portraits.

James Gates Percival

1823. Oil on millboard, 15½ x 11⅞"
Collection of Mr. and Mrs. Robert D. Schwarz,
Philadelphia

In a letter to Percival of June 11, 1823, James Yvonnet remarked that Morse's "face is good,—not handsome, but lighted up and intellectual. Have I hit it right?" To which Percival replied, "I have lately had some intimacy with Morse, while taking a portrait of my phiz. Your judgment is not far from correct. He is a good artist, and has a mind much above the common level." Percival (1795–1856) was the unhappy editor of the Connecticut Herald *from February to June, 1823, and a lady who knew him well at this time noted that he "was very eccentric, and I think at last deranged."*

David Curtis DeForest

1823. Oil on canvas, 35 x 28″
Yale University Art Gallery,
New Haven, Connecticut
Gift of Mrs. P. J. Griffin

Both of Morse's portraits of DeForest (1774–1825) decisively grasp the hauteur of the man whose troublesome activities (for government policy) in South America led John Quincy Adams to characterize him as "cunning and deceptive."

This reason is not to make himself younger, but to appear to children and grandchildren more suitably matched as to age with their mother and grandmother.

If Mr. Morse is at leisure and disposed to undertake this work, he will please prepare his canvas and let me know when he is ready for my attendance.

David Curtis DeForest, imperious and wealthy, had run away to sea as a boy and later served as a U.S. naval officer. Abruptly leaving his ship in 1801 in South America, he settled in Buenos Aires and established the first commercial trading between the United States and Argentina. When he was thirty-seven, he married fifteen-year-old Julia Wooster of Huntington, Connecticut, and they subsequently divided their time between New Haven and Buenos Aires. Now forty-nine, he was sensitive about the increasingly apparent age gap between them, which prompted his request to Morse.

Mrs. David Curtis DeForest

1823. Oil on canvas, 35 x 28"
Yale University Art Gallery,
New Haven, Connecticut
Gift of Mrs. P. J. Griffin

Still only seventeen years old when she was presented to President Monroe in December, 1819, Julia Wooster DeForest (c. 1795/96–1873) on that occasion wore the elegant gown commemorated in this portrait. That her gown and her coiffure overwhelm her rather bland expression may be attributed to her husband's vanity rather than her own.

There are two portraits of DeForest. One is a pendant to his wife's, the other a single image now in Buenos Aires. The single portrait was probably painted slightly earlier; he presented it to the University of Buenos Aires, of which he was one of the principal founding benefactors. The rejuvenated likeness, on the other hand, was a "social" portrait for his New Haven friends, as well as his children. Poor Morse must have had unsettling memories of General Stark and son and wondered how many more times he would have to add or subtract years from a sitter's appearance.

In the summer of 1823 in New Haven, while still working on the marble-carving machine mentioned earlier, Morse mused, "I could easily be a sculptor." Indeed he could have been, as his small *Hercules* had demonstrated. During these months he probably painted the Percival portrait and small individual likenesses of his parents.

Reverend Jedidiah Morse

c. 1823. Oil on panel, 10 x 8″
Courtesy of The Harvard University Art
Museums (Fogg Art Museum),
Cambridge, Massachusetts
Bequest of Grenville L. Winthrop

The man who was described by Daniel Webster as "always thinking, always writing, always talking, always acting," is seen in a more reposeful old age. The Calvinist severity of his earlier portraits is replaced by the candid expression of an honest, intelligent, tolerant man. His plain-spoken wife once reproved his charitable attitude toward some hostile parishioners: "Mr. Morse, charity is not a fool."

The portraits of his parents, the last records Samuel made of them, are as gentle as they are painterly. Both may be unfinished, as has been suggested, but they are complete for their purpose. They are familial gifts, lovingly presented. The features, especially Jedidiah's, are softened by time and a son's love. Ill and without a pulpit, the elderly pastor has clearly lost none of his principles. His head is thinly painted; the hair seems floated rather than brushed on, but sharply brushed accents at his temple and above his left eye convey the still vigorous intellect. His wife looks equally dignified. Though her portrait is more descriptive, the nearly frontal face, strongly framed by bonnet and collar, remains the reposeful focus of the painting.

But family portraits earned no income. In the middle of August Morse set

Mrs. Jedidiah Morse

c. 1823. Oil on panel, 10 x 8"
Courtesy of the Harvard University Art
Museums (Fogg Art Museum),
Cambridge, Massachusetts.
Bequest of Grenville L. Winthrop

out once more in search of commissions. In Albany the promise of much patronage dwindled to the reality of three portraits, one a gift. Nonetheless, it was there
that he observed that the Erie Canal was destined to bring increased wealth to
New York, which made him consider moving permanently to New York City to
position himself for future patronage. "It will be advantageous to me to be previously identified among her citizens as a painter. It requires some little time to
become known in such a city as N. York." With only a brief stopover in New Haven, Morse went from Albany to New York in September.

His brothers had preceded him. At the beginning of 1823, Sidney, assisted
by Richard, had founded a religious weekly, the *New-York Observer*. Their com-
panionship and the introductions they could supply were welcome. Samuel

rented a studio on Broadway opposite the Trinity Churchyard and advertised his presence in his brothers' paper. His first subject—in November—was apparently James Kent, then about to retire as chancellor of the New York Court of Chancery to resume his position as professor of law at Columbia. He was not a good sitter. "He is very impatient and you well know that I cannot paint an impatient person; I must have my mind at ease or I cannot paint." Since no further portrait commissions were forthcoming, he painted at least one now unlocated scene from Washington Irving's *Sketch Book*, "Ichabod Crane and the Headless Horseman."

Morse's mind was never idle when work was slow, and he soon conceived a *"secret scheme."* The government intended to send its first ambassador to Mexico. He wrote to friends in Congress, including Robert Young Hayne and Joel Poinsett (the likely choice as minister), applying for some position in the legation that would allow him to go "free of expense and under government protection," with the understanding that he would continue painting while discharging his duties as attaché. He recalled that the great Peter Paul Rubens had successfully combined the professions of artist and diplomat. Privately Morse also expressed his intention to exhibit his *House of Representatives*, "which, in the present state of favorable feeling towards our country, I should probably dispose of to advantage." His petition was approved by President Monroe; he returned to New Haven, whence his wife, children, and father accompanied him as far as New York. " 'Farewell, farewell' seemed written on the very walls," wrote Morse, who then went once again to Washington, in April, 1824, to await the final preparations for his departure to Mexico.

Chancellor James Kent

1823. Oil on canvas, 30 x 25"
William Rockhill Nelson Gallery of Art,
Kansas City, Missouri

The dour appearance of Kent (1763–1847) fronted a keen legal mind. His court decisions were among the most formative of the Federal period of U.S. history, and his Commentaries on American Law *confirmed his reputation.*

THE NATIONAL HALL

Chancellor James Kent

VI. "Promoting the Arts"

IN WASHINGTON, PLANS FOR THE MEXICAN MISSION soon soured. The minister-designate, Congressman Ninian Edwards of Illinois, made some ill-advised charges against a prominent presidential hopeful, Secretary of the Treasury William H. Crawford. In the resulting political uproar, Edwards was persuaded to resign the post, and the Mexican mission was indefinitely postponed. By then Morse had already returned to New Haven, and by June had resumed his itinerant search for portrait commissions. The summer of 1824 found him in New Brunswick, New Jersey, and Hartford, Connecticut; in Concord (where Lucretia and the children were visiting her parents) and Portsmouth, New Hampshire; and in Portland, Maine.

Either in Concord that summer or earlier in the year in New Haven, Morse painted an unusual portrait, *Lucretia Morse and Her Children*. The imaginative composition derives from Renaissance imagery such as the Madonna and Child, or Charity (*caritas*), already borrowed and reinterpreted in portraits by Joshua Reynolds and other English painters. The palette is especially striking. Darker tones of purplish brown and olive green and the cerulean blue sky to the left of the shadowed column are used to set off thinly brushed gold and yellow, soft blues and candy pinks, and creamy white. Creamy, indeed! The picture was painted, he told Daniel Huntington, "with colors ground in milk, and the effect was juicy, creamy, and pearly to a degree." It demonstrated, said Huntington, that "Morse's love of scientific experiments was shown in his artist life."

In Hartford, Eliphalet Terry commissioned portraits of himself and his wife. A prominent export grocer, Terry had become a director of the young Hartford Fire Insurance Company in 1819 and later was named its president. Both technically and formally, these portraits exhibit the artist's sure command of his expressive means. The paintings are as poised and assured as their subjects. Direct and candid, devoid of pomposity, they testify to a meeting of minds between the artist and his sitters.

In New Haven, the architect George Hoadley asked Morse to paint Eli Whitney, thus making possible the historical oddity of a painting of one famous inventor by another famous inventor. The frontal bluntness of the self-made man is reminiscent of the earlier portrait of the cabinetmaker Alexander Calder. In both, the simple color scheme, broad forms, and psychological immediacy are outstanding. The slanted pose and the skillfully modeled face of Whitney convey an alert intelligence and a thinly veiled impatience.

Lucretia Morse and Her Children

c. 1824. Oil on canvas, 40 x 36"
Private collection

An aura of melancholy pervades this painting despite, or perhaps because of, the lively pose of young Charles. His mother called the frail child "little Charles," and her solicitude is apparent in glance and gesture. With touching eagerness, he stretches his hands toward the soap bubbles—symbols of the fragility of human life—which Susan Morse has blown. It is significant that Morse's first sketch for the painting (now lost) showed Susan with a book. The substitution of the pipe and bubbles betrays his fears for his son. The pale palette further enhances the tender, apprehensive mood.

88

Lucretia Morse and Her Children

Lydia Coit Terry

c. 1824. Oil on canvas, 29¾ x 24¾"
National Gallery of Art, Washington, D.C.
Gift of Dr. Charles Terry Butler

The date assigned to these portraits depends upon circumstantial evidence. A descendant of the Terrys discovered a piece of lace from a cap, "which was worn, according to a notation ... by Lydia while sitting for her portrait in 1824." Lydia Coit (1788–1831) was Terry's second wife. She died in childbirth after fourteen years of marriage.

Morse's portraits of that summer are strong, mature works; how much more, therefore, must the demeaning status of the itinerant artist have rankled him. He gave voice to his irritation in a letter from Portland (August 10, 1824): "I arrived here on Saturday, bringing three letters from gentlemen in Portsmouth to General Wingate, Judge Mellen, and Mr. Asa Clapp. . . . I find that General W. and his lady leave tomorrow for Boston. Judge Mellen and family are absent on a tour, and I only find Mr. Clapp, who has no more taste than a cow."

Returning to New York in the fall, he launched himself into New York society with the help of old New Haven friends like the younger James Hillhouse. He developed the acquaintance of one of the most notable personalities of the era: Philip Hone, then forty-four, self-made like Terry and Whitney, with a fortune from the auction business. Acquiring cultivation with his wealth, Hone began to buy books and pictures. Always deeply con-

Avoiding all ostentation, Morse concentrates on the shrewd character of the Yankee businessman, conveyed especially by the uneven placement of the eyes and the strong, aquiline nose. As president of the Hartford Fire Insurance Company, Terry (1776–1849) saw to it that every claim was paid in full following the calamitous New York City fire of December 17, 1835, saving the firm from bankruptcy and greatly enhancing its reputation and future success.

cerned with New York and national politics, he served one term as mayor in 1825. Hone owned one version of Morse's 1823 portrait of Chancellor Kent, which may have occasioned their meeting, and he probably introduced Morse to his brother, Isaac, who now ran the family business.

Morse's portrait of Isaac's five-year-old daughter, known to us as *Little Miss Hone*, is surely one of the most atypical works of his career. Perhaps the nature of the auction house, with its characteristic jumble of household goods, foodstuffs, and paintings, influenced the idiosyncratic nature of Morse's picture. In addition to the Empire settee and pedestal table, the elaborate pilaster of a fireplace, and the velvet hat, the painting originally included pictures on the wall and "an ugly carpet on the floor" (this according to a previous owner who had the picture cut down to "improve" the effect!).

Its sweet tenderness recalls English sentimental portraits of children by Thomas Gainsborough and others. When that sensibility is combined with the

Eli Whitney

c. 1824. Oil on canvas, 35⅝ x 27¾"
Yale University Art Gallery,
New Haven, Connecticut
Gift of George Hoadley, B.A. 1801

In the presence of Morse's Whitney, *one feels the artist's special affinity for sitters of restless intellect and imagination, whose drive to succeed and to influence others sometimes made them figures of contention—like Morse himself. Like Morse later, Whitney (1765–1825) spent considerable time and energy on the securing and protecting of patents.*

Little Miss Hone

1824. Oil on panel, 30 x 25"
Museum of Fine Arts, Boston

"I am engaged in painting the full-length portrait of Mr. Hone's little daughter, a pretty little girl just as old as Susan. I have made a sketch of the composition with which I am pleased, and so are the father and mother. I shall paint her with a cat set up in her lap like a baby, with a towel under its chin and a cap on its head, and she employed in feeding it with a spoon" (December 5, 1824).

elaborate setting, the painting seems to us proto-Victorian. Morse's penchant for an unusual palette shows itself again. Muted and pleasant, the colors include pale mauve, wine purple, pink, yellow, and blue-green, accounting for the picture's true charm.

Morse took some pupils-cum-assistants at this time, specifically "Mr. Agate and Mr. Field, [who] are very tractable and very useful." The latter was Erastus Salisbury Field, then nineteen, whose apprenticeship with Morse lasted about fourteen months and constituted the sole formal instruction this memorable Massachusetts naive artist ever received. Frederick Agate later assisted his mentor in founding the National Academy of Design.

As 1824 ended, Morse clearly felt that at last his career was truly launched: "I am going on prosperously through the kindness of Providence

Little Miss Hone

Marquis de Lafayette

1825–26. Oil on canvas, 96 x 64"
Courtesy of Art Commission of the
City of New York, City Hall

*If Morse's pose for the marquis recalls his
earlier portrait of President Monroe, both
of them probably have a common model in
Joshua Reynolds's great portrait of Frederick Howard, 5th Earl of Carlisle (1769,
Castle Howard). Reynolds's source, it is
generally agreed, is the* Apollo Belvedere. *That Morse would have seen this as
an appropriate model for his hero is suggested by Friedrich von Schiller's 1795
description of the sculpture's "celestial
mixture of accessibility and severity, be-
nevolence and gravity, majesty and mild-
ness," an evocation that is astonishingly
apt for Morse's* Lafayette.

in raising up many friends who are exerting themselves in my favor. My
storms are partly over, and a clear and pleasant day is dawning upon me."
Though his forecast was to prove flawed, 1825 was indeed to be a year he
would never forget.

At the beginning of January, Morse received his most important commission since the full-length portrait of President Monroe. From among the lead-

ing portraitists of the day—including Charles Ingham, John Wesley Jarvis, Thomas Sully, and Rembrandt Peale—the Common Council of the City of New York chose Morse to paint a full-length of the Marquis de Lafayette (for which he expected to receive one thousand dollars). It was the preeminent portrait commission of the decade. Lafayette's arrival in New York in August, 1824, marked the beginning of a triumphant curtain call for the "Hero of Two Worlds" that lasted thirteen months and took him as far as Cincinnati. As one of the last survivors of the Revolution he had done so much to advance, his tour was greeted with a passionate outpouring of gratitude unprecedented in America. It was again as a French contemporary had remarked forty years earlier: "It is impossible to be more generally loved throughout the United States than M. le marquis de La Fayette."

On January 20, 1825, Lucretia gave birth to their third child, Finley, but Morse was forced to delay his return to New Haven until he could go to Washington to take Lafayette's likeness. He reached the capital on February 7, presented himself to the marquis the next day, and was overwhelmed to realize that this was "the man whose beloved name has run from one end of this continent to the other, whom all flock to see, whom all delight to honor; this is the man, the very identical man!"

He had two or three sittings in the next three days but was "much perplexed for want of time; I mean *his time*. He is so harassed by visitors and has so many letters to write that I find it exceedingly difficult to do the subject justice." Another sitting or two were deferred until that summer in New York. He wrote another letter to Lucretia on the tenth. In it he described his attendance at President Monroe's last reception at the White House and Lafayette's charming introduction of him as "Mr. Morse, the painter, the son of the geographer; he has come to Washington to take the topography of my face."

At this gratifying moment Morse could not know that his beloved wife, only twenty-five, had died suddenly, apparently of unsuspected heart disease, at about the same hour he had arrived in Washington. He learned of the tragedy on the eleventh and left immediately for New Haven, though he arrived after the burial. He was inconsolable but returned to New York with his eldest child, Susan, and immersed himself in the great project at hand. In later life he always associated the portrait with his devastating loss, and it may be that some of the passion of the Lafayette portrait flows from the deep emotions tapped by Morse's sorrow.

Once more Samuel Morse had the happy opportunity to paint a symbolic image. The heroic sublimity of the portrait derives from the bold simplicity of composition and color, which embody the ideal of noble magnanimity, rather than from any overtly dramatic action. The low viewpoint and closely placed feet create an upward surge of energy through the hieratically motionless figure. To Lafayette's right are busts of Washington and Franklin, long-dead comrades in revolution. The third pedestal is vacant; it is destined for Lafayette's bust, and he, a living monument, rests his hand upon it. A species of helianthus (which turns always toward the sun) rises from an urn at his left—

Marquis de Lafayette

1825. Oil on canvas, 30 x 25"
The New York Public Library
Astor, Lenox and Tilden Foundations

This life study of Lafayette (1757–1834) was painted in Washington in February. The distinctive features are strongly grasped. Modeling with energetic strokes of color, Morse paints the face in broad outline and emphatic planes. Though the marquis has a vigor that belies his sixty-eight years, it is a realistic head. It was soon acquired by Philip Hone, who, as mayor of New York in 1825, was a member of the Lafayette reception committee.

an emblem of the hero's "noble firmness and consistency" to his principles, which Morse saw "strongly indicated in his whole face." While the glowing evening sky may refer to the twilight of the hero's life, this and the landscape below also betoken an Arcadian paradise, a serene assurance of the nation's future.

It is not known if there was an intended location for Morse's painting, but it should be noted that the heroic portrait commissioned by the city just before the *Lafayette* was John Vanderlyn's *Andrew Jackson* (1823). They are the same size, and Morse may have intended to contrast the battle scene behind Vanderlyn's hero with the peaceful landscape behind Lafayette, signifying the unfolding of an era of peace and prosperity as America neared its fiftieth birthday. Whether viewed symbolically or simply as the memorable depiction of a great man, Morse's *Marquis de Lafayette* is his highest achievement in portraiture.

Other portraits occupied Morse at the same time, including those of Yale professors Dr. Nathan Smith and Benjamin Silliman. No person had exercised a greater influence on Morse's scientific curiosity than Silliman, whom he had now known nearly twenty years, since his first studies with him at Yale. As the founder in 1818 and for many years sole editor of the influential *American Journal of Science and Arts* (often called "Silliman's Journal"), and as a lucid and enthralling lecturer at Yale and to the lay public for half a century, Silliman had an unequaled impact on American science. He and Morse had continued as friends, and Silliman later supported him in his development and defense of the telegraph. Silliman had composed the epitaph for Lucretia's tombstone. Soon thereafter Morse was apparently commissioned by the Yale Class of 1825 to paint Silliman's portrait. The sittings were in New York, and on July 13 Morse wrote to his parents, "I expect to finish Prof. Silliman's Picture this week so as to be able to bring it with me to N. Haven on Saturday. . . . I have been wholly occupied in running after Lafayette."

Silliman's colleagues thought that the impassive countenance was not a good likeness. Although it is a large and imposing composition, the portrait is intentionally unanimated. Unintentionally it also lacks the vitality that courses through the *Lafayette*. This may be an accurate record of Silliman's "depressed state of health," because of which he later recalled: "The delicate languor of the portrait was then in the original." (Silliman was referring to Trumbull's likeness, painted at the same time.)

Still, Morse's idealism must be remembered. As with *The House of Representatives*, his audience failed to realize that he was preoccupied with infusing portraiture with the intellectual and moral qualities associated with history painting. Silliman's portrait has accurately been called an "icon of learning" by William H. Gerdts, and the array of mineral specimens, the lectern, and the view of West Rock near New Haven all contribute to this interpretation. The minerals refer to the George Gibbs mineral collection, which Silliman obtained for Yale in 1823; he had discussed the geology of West Rock in an article of 1806; the lectern estab-

Benjamin Silliman

1825. Oil on canvas, 55¼ x 44¼"
Yale University Art Gallery,
New Haven, Connecticut
Gift of Bartlett Arkell to Silliman College

It is ironic that just as the rivalry between Morse and John Trumbull was about to become public, both artists were simultaneously painting portraits of Silliman. In a late memoir he recalled that he sat for Trumbull from six to seven-thirty in the morning at his rooms near City Hall, then after breakfast went to Morse's new home "uptown" in Canal Street, where he remained until ten o'clock. "Col. Trumbull painted very rapidly—Mr. Morse was less rapid and both were very agreeable companions." Silliman (1779–1864) was related to Trumbull by marriage, was responsible for the acquisition of the artist's paintings by Yale (in exchange for an annuity), made possible the building of the Trumbull Gallery, and served as its curator.

Benjamin Silliman

Professor Nathan Smith, M.D.

1825. Oil on canvas, 43⅝ x 34″
Yale University Art Gallery,
New Haven, Connecticut
Gift of the Medical Class of 1826 to the
School of Medicine

Morse received this commission at the same time as the Lafayette, though this one would bring him only a hundred dollars. The composition is closely related to one of Gilbert Stuart's favorite inventions, used, for example, in his portrait of Thomas Jefferson (Bowdoin College). But within this convention Morse poses his sitter with greater vigor than does Stuart. The compact torso has a tightly coiled power that seems barely contained by the counter-curves of chair and curtain. His gaze is riveting and austere. Smith (1762–1829), one of the most progressive physicians of his day, was the founder of Dartmouth's medical school and, despite his Harvard (and Unitarian) background, taught at Yale for most of his career.

lishes him as a professor while also alluding to the pulpit. Morse was aware that Silliman had developed a personal synthesis of scientific objectivity and divine creation, and it is not incidental that the pose here is most nearly related to that of Reverend Nathaniel Bowen in Morse's earlier portrait.

Although it is often said that Silliman is shown lecturing, he clearly is not. He is posing, silent and motionless, and there is no suggestion of an audience. The most unusual feature of the pose is the placement, exactly in the center of the painting, of the right hand and the mineral it holds. Here it departs, somewhat awkwardly, from otherwise similar prototypes. It may be that this mineral held some special significance for Silliman. The handsome still life of minerals and other objects on the table and lectern, incidentally, is rare in Morse's work.

Among the other portraits of 1825, that of William Cullen Bryant is especially memorable. He knew Bryant as a member of the Bread and Cheese Club, the first important social club in New York, founded in 1824 by James Fenimore Cooper. Although it was nominally a writers' club, its members—the so-called Knickerbockers—were artists and amateurs as well. Besides Bryant and Morse, these included William Dunlap, John Wesley Jarvis, James Kent, and Philip and Isaac Hone.

Morse's softly romantic portrait of Bryant combines reverie with a firmly grasped reality. The natural flesh tones and the carefully modeled, strongly lit brow give the man substance and firm intelligence; the landscape with trees and evening sky seen dimly through the window strikes the poetic note. Morse is very close to Allston in his conception; the latter's portrait of Samuel Taylor Coleridge, like Morse's *Bryant*, conveys the poet's genius through romantic mood rather than with external props and symbols.

In 1824 Morse had been elected an honorary member of the American Academy of the Fine Arts, founded in 1802 (as the New York Academy of Fine Arts), which had gradually become as conservative as it was powerful. This power stemmed from its tacit control of much of New York's available patronage, since the board was composed almost entirely of prominent lay citizens who were also the prime buyers of art. Although an artist, Colonel John Trumbull, who became president of the academy in 1816, proved reactionary, and the institution became increasingly less democratic and less responsive to artists' needs.

Although Morse and Trumbull held each other in mutual, if grudging, respect, they had always been potential rivals. As early as August, 1823, Morse had written privately: "Colonel T. is growing old, and there is no artist of education sufficiently prominent to take his place as President of the Academy of Arts. By becoming more known to the New York public, and exerting my talents to discover the best methods of promoting the Arts and writing about them, I may possibly be promoted to his place, where I could have a better opportunity of doing *something for the arts of our country*, the object at which I aim."

These ambitious sentiments were followed by Morse's rapid rise to artistic eminence in New York, culminating in his *Lafayette* commission. The latter must have really rankled the colonel, who had been aide to General Washington and was an old acquaintance of the marquis. Nonetheless, Morse exhibited his *House of Representatives* at the Academy's spring exhibition in 1825 and generally was at pains to remain on good terms with Trumbull and the board.

The situation changed unexpectedly and radically that fall when two students, Thomas Cummings and Frederick Agate (Morse's apprentice), arrived at the Academy's rooms to draw from casts and found the studio locked when it should have been open. They complained and were put in their place by Trumbull himself with the gratuitous remark, "Beggars are not to be choosers." Cummings described the ensuing events:

On the 8th of November, 1825, a meeting of the Artists, probably the first ever held in the city, took place . . . for the purpose of taking into consideration "the formation of a Society for

Improvement in Drawing." Mr. Durand was called to the chair, and Mr. Morse was appointed Secretary.

The question of organization was put, and carried unanimously; and the so associated artists were from thenceforth to be known as the "NEW-YORK DRAWING ASSOCIATION." Samuel F. B. Morse was chosen to preside over its meetings. . . . It was entirely distinct from the American Academy of Arts, and probably would ever have remained so without organizing a new Academy, had it not been for the interference of the President of the American. . . . After all the insult that had been heaped on the artists . . . [they] were no sooner organized than they were claimed as STUDENTS of the AMERICAN Academy.

On one of the drawing evenings in December, 1825, Colonel Trumbull . . . entered the room in which the associated artists were drawing . . . and looking authoritatively around . . . producing the matriculation-book of the American Academy, he requested that it should be signed by all, as students of that Institution. . . . The Colonel waited some time, but receiving neither compliance nor attention, left in the same stately manner he had entered. . . .

This extraordinary performance was still insufficient to provoke the dissident artists to form a new academy, in no small part because they were loath to antagonize the board, i.e., the art patrons. Thus they endeavored to negotiate a compromise that would bring artists into a position of approximate parity. The directors treated the dissidents contemptuously, "proclaimed that 'Artists were unfit to manage an Academy'—'that they were always *quarreling*'; and concluded with the words, 'Colonel Trumbull says so.' "

His was not the last say-so, however. On January 14, 1826, at a meeting of the New-York Drawing Association, Morse declared: "We have this evening assumed a new attitude in the community: our negotiations with the Academy are at an end; our union with it has been frustrated, after every proper effort on our part to accomplish it." The resolutions offered that night established the National Academy of Design. If "national" seemed presumptuous for a fledgling local institution, it was candidly explained by Cummings: "Any less name than National would be taking one below the American Academy. . . . If we were simply the Associated Artists, their name would swallow us up."

The National Academy seems to have been born of communal sentiment among the protesting artists, with no undue influence of ringleaders or rabble-rousers. Nonetheless, when Morse assumed its presidency in 1826, he did so with force and clarity of purpose. He led the National Academy for twenty years and in that position willingly waded into the politics of art in order to "*do something for the arts of our country*"—an aim he assuredly realized.

Incredibly, in the space of one year, Samuel F. B. Morse had gained a third child, lost his precious wife, painted his most renowned portrait, established himself as New York's leading painter, and founded an art academy. The vertiginous course of his life from January, 1825, through January, 1826, seems appalling to us: triumph canceled by tragedy, success when he had no Lucretia with whom to share it. Whatever its source, Morse's steadfastness is astonishing. We must remember that he was only thirty-four, not the later patriarch whose appearance is so familiar to us. Ironically, from its inception the National Academy of Design

William Cullen Bryant

1825. Oil on canvas, 30 x 24⅞″
National Academy of Design, New York

Although his fame as a poet was established with the publication of Thanatopsis *when he was twenty-three, Bryant (1794–1878) was as well known to his contemporaries as the editor of the New York* Evening Post *beginning in 1829. The antislavery views expressed there were a factor in the founding of the Republican party, although Bryant was a Democrat. His political enemies, such as Philip Hone, found his editorials "virulent and malignant. . . . How such a blackhearted misanthrope . . . should possess an imagination teeming with beautiful poetical images astonishes me."*

PROMOTING THE ARTS

William Cullen Bryant

De Witt Clinton

was so popular among artists and patrons that his duties increasingly prevented Morse from meeting the increased demand for his portraits. At the time the controversy began he was, as Cummings later put it, "in the enjoyment of lucrative and prosperous practice." After the founding of the National Academy, he often sent prospective sitters to other artists, and his patronage "never fully returned to him."

At the beginning of 1826, however, Morse undertook the portrait of a man who had more than a passing interest in the conflict between the American Academy and the National Academy. Governor De Witt Clinton, an old friend of Jedidiah Morse, is remembered today as the champion of the Erie Canal ("Clinton's Big Ditch"). The role of the canal in the economic development of New York City had been anticipated by Samuel Morse in 1823 when he visited Albany. But Clinton was also a champion of the arts and sciences; he had advanced the argument that some of the revenues from state-sponsored canals should be expended "in encouraging the arts and sciences . . . [and] in fostering the inventions of genius." As past president of the American Academy, his liberalizing intentions for that institution had been stymied by Trumbull's conservatism. His sympathy for the new academy is inherent in his sitting for its president, although he did so at the request of the engraver Moseley I. Danforth, another of the original founders. Danforth's intended engraving of the painting was never made.

That Morse sensed which way the wind was blowing even before the rebellion at the American Academy of the Fine Arts is made abundantly clear by his "Lectures on the Affinity of Painting with the Other Fine Arts." Although they were delivered in March and April of 1826, they were already in preparation at the beginning of November, 1825, as part of a series of lectures under the aegis of the recently founded New York Athenaeum. Even more, perhaps, than his administrative responsibilities at the National Academy or his portrait commissions, these lectures consumed his time and energy—"every leisure moment." "These lectures are of great importance to me, for, if well done, they place me alone among the artists; I being the only one who has yet written a course of lectures in our country. Time bestowed on them is not, therefore, misspent, for they will acquire me reputation which will yield wealth."

Morse's emphasis on the possible financial rewards of intellectual pursuit was by now reflexive: he had been unable to support his family in their own home, and now his wife was dead; his debts were considerable despite his growing renown; his family thought him incapable of managing his finances. Even now, when his reputation had reached new heights, brother Sidney wrote to brother Richard: "Finley is well and in good spirits, though not advancing very rapidly in his business. He is full of the Academy and of his lectures—can hardly talk on any other subject. I despair of ever seeing him rich or even at ease in his pecuniary circumstances from efforts of his own, though able to do it with so little effort."

In due course the lectures were a huge success, which Sidney reported to their parents: "His lectures have done him great credit & bro't the arts into more estimation." William Dunlap recorded that the series "was received by crowded

De Witt Clinton

1826. Oil on canvas, 30 x 25⅛"
Metropolitan Museum of Art, Rogers Fund, 1909

Clinton (1769–1828) is shown at the apex of his career. He had opened the Erie Canal in 1825, and his popularity was enormous. Morse expertly conveys the pugnacious tenacity of the governor's Irish heritage by the turn of the florid head, the set of the jaw, and the sturdy, thickset torso. The flashing eyes also reflect Clinton's Irish humor, the "moments of ease and hilarity" recalled by Philip Hone, "when he laid aside his state to be a boy once more." The red brocade background has a repeated emblem with the initial "C" set within a star and encircled by a laurel wreath to proclaim the governor's fame.

audiences with delight." It was generally recognized that Morse was the only American artist with sufficient erudition to have even attempted such a wide-ranging topic. But historically significant though they were in the context of American art, the lectures (as Nicolai Cikovsky, Jr., has observed) "were persuasive and pedagogical, designed to educate the public about established artistic and critical beliefs, not to assail such beliefs or to concoct new ones." Essentially retrospective, they appealed neither to American chauvinism nor to European snobbism, and they made no appeal for "modernism." For an American audience, Morse reiterated the age-old European argument for painting as a liberal, intellectual art. In short, the lectures were more closely related to the art he wished to practice than to that he did practice.

His own portraits had never been finer than during 1826, although that of Lafayette remained unfinished until the summer. "I have many times resolved to let everything else suffer and finish it, but some unforeseen event has from the very commencement constantly broken in, and obliged me to delay it" (May 10). His father's final illness—he had been in declining health since the preparation of his Indian report—called Morse to New Haven, where Jedidiah died on June 9. Returning to New York, he finished the *Lafayette* in a few weeks, and it was delivered to City Hall. Now the portrait was linked in his mind to two deaths in his family.

Perhaps the fact that the great work remained in his studio for half of 1826 stimulated the high quality of other portraits of that year. In any case, the paired portraits of the Honorable Stephen Mix Mitchell and Mrs. Stephen Mix (Hannah Grant) Mitchell of Wethersfield, Connecticut, are among the most memorable of his career. Again, Morse demonstrates his profound sympathy with aged sitters. Viewed side by side, they are the embodiment of kinship. Benevolent yet forceful, both heads lean in the same direction, at the same angle, in the unconscious congruence born of fifty-seven years of marriage. Within that union Morse subtly differentiates their characters. The judge's face, its features kneaded with bunches and pinches of paint, pushes forward attentively. The upswept crest of his wig and the energetic design of his cravat contribute to the quiet power of this impressive man. In contrast, his wife's features seem etched or carved into the paint, and the simple disposition of her shawl in parallel curves contributes to an aura of repose, without masking her shrewd intelligence.

The 1827 spring exhibition of the National Academy should have been a triumph for Morse. He showed his *House of Representatives*, the *Lafayette*, and the portrait of Judge Mitchell (possibly also that of Mrs. Mitchell as *Portrait of a Lady*). Moreover, these proofs of his ability appeared as the aged Gilbert Stuart was passing from the scene, leaving only Sully as serious competition among portrait painters. On May 3 he gave a much-noted lecture, "Academies of Art," which surveyed the history of European academies and suggested that the National Academy was the American heir to the great tradition in art, with the distinction of its being a democratic institution that depended upon "the constant action and reaction of the artists and the public upon each other." He was also a writer for the *Observer*, his brothers' paper, and conceived and founded a new paper of

William Paulding

Honorable Stephen Mix Mitchell

1826. Oil on canvas, 29¾ x 24¾"
The Connecticut Historical Society, Hartford

The venerable Judge Mitchell (1743–1835) at eighty-two could survey a distinguished career when he sat to Morse in New York. A Yale graduate, he practiced law, was elected to the state legislature and the U.S. Senate, was a delegate to the Continental Congress, and held several judicial posts, retiring as chief justice of the State of Connecticut in 1814.

moral commentary, the *Journal of Commerce*, though the fact remained a family secret: "It is important on every account at present that I should be unknown." (He must have felt the spotlight of controversy a little too bright.)

With all this, he often felt "desponding in consequence of having no commissions for pictures, I am absolutely entirely without anything to paint for anyone . . . and I am at a loss almost what course to pursue" (March 20). The business he had given to others was now regretted. One commission of 1826—*Una and the Dwarf*, a subject drawn from Edmund Spenser's *Faerie Queene* (1590)—was probably not completed until after the 1827 exhibition. This departure from his portrait practice was owed to James A. Stevens, owner of a steamboat company, who ordered thirteen landscapes and historical subjects to decorate his new Hudson River steamboat *Albany*. Morse was one of seven artists, including

Thomas Cole, Thomas Sully, and John Vanderlyn, enlisted for the project. Although the paintings were to be mounted as the paneling of a gallery in the manner of decorative mural painting, Morse wrote his mother that he considered "this as a new and noble channel for the encouragement of painting, and in such an enterprise and in such company I shall do my best."

It is probably not coincidental that this letter immediately continues with thoughts of returning to Europe "to visit Paris and Rome to finish what I began before" (November 9, 1826). For in 1813, while in London, Morse had written to a friend: "The little time that I can spare from painting I employ in reading and studying the old poets, Spenser, Chaucer, Dante, Tasso, etc. These are necessary to a painter." That they had never proved necessary until now must have rankled the would-be history painter anew.

Mrs. Stephen Mix Mitchell

1826. Oil on canvas, 29¾ x 24¾"
The Connecticut Historical Society, Hartford

Hannah Grant Mitchell (1748–1830) was the daughter of a Scotsman, whose diligence had enabled her to bring a considerable fortune to the union. To this she added, as Morse's portrait reveals, a considerable intelligence and strength of character. The right side of her face is fully lit, as is the left side of her husband's. Since the light unites them, it seems clear that her portrait was intended to hang to the right of his.

Una and the Dwarf

1827. Oil on wood, 26⅚₆ x 47⅞"
Toledo Museum of Art, Ohio

The hero of Spenser's Faerie Queene, *the Red Cross Knight, has been seduced by a witch and imprisoned by a giant. The dwarf, his page, has brought his master's armor to the spiritually pure Una, and together they lament him. Prince Arthur arrives providentially, the dwarf points to the castle where the Red Cross Knight is imprisoned, and Arthur subsequently rescues him. Morse chooses to stress the sentimental moral of steadfast devotion rather than a passage of heroic action. It is a synthesis of passages from Book I, canto vii, stanzas 19–52, except for the dwarf's gesture, which comes from canto viii, stanza 2.*

Jonas Platt

1827–28. Oil on canvas, 36¼ x 29½"
The Brooklyn Museum, New York
Dick S. Ramsay Fund

A son of the founder of Plattsburgh, New York, Platt (1769–1834) studied law in New York City and served in Congress and the state legislature. As a state senator he introduced the bill proposing the Erie Canal project. The painting is subtle and accomplished, particularly in the modeling of the face, the exquisite veining of the hands, and the transition between figure and background.

Spenser's epic poem was as popular with English-speaking readers and painters of the eighteenth and nineteenth century as it is unread today; both circumstances can be attributed to its allegorical, moralizing intent. Although heroic virtue is admirable, it may also be dull unless accompanied by action. But Morse, predictably, avoids the dramatic, intentionally choosing the static, descriptive passage between dramatic events. In contrast, when his mentor Washington Allston turned to the *Faerie Queene*, he illustrated the *Flight of Florimell*—at once vivid, romantic, and mysterious.

The Athenaeum lecture schedule for January and February of 1827 included Professor James Freeman Dana of Columbia College, speaking on the subject of electromagnetism. Morse attended, and his collegiate interest in the subject was renewed. In the few months before Dana's death in April, Morse was brought up to date on advances in the science—knowledge that would soon find a new application in his imagination.

Morse escaped from the city's summer heat by visiting relatives and acquaintances in upstate New York. At their home in Sconandoa, near Utica, he painted a pair of small but brilliant portraits of his aunt and uncle, Mr. and Mrs. Samuel Sidney Breese. Either during that summer (perhaps at Whitesboro) or back in New York, he painted two portraits of his friend Jonas Platt. The larger of the two was commissioned by their mutual friend, Moss Kent, the chancellor's brother. The frontality and impassivity of the figure are reminiscent of the *Benjamin Silliman*, as is the relative complexity of the painting.

As 1828 began, the relations between the National Academy of Design and its arthritic elder, the American Academy of the Fine Arts, became more unpleasant and very public. Morse's lecture, "Academies of Art," had been published, and in January John Trumbull's critical response to it appeared in the *North American Review*. In the same periodical a month later Morse responded to

Jonas Platt

*Mrs. Samuel Sidney Breese
(née Helena Burrows)*

1827. Oil on wood, 16½ x 12⅝"
Yale University Art Gallery,
New Haven, Connecticut
Gift of the Associates in Fine Arts

*A blue-eyed beauty, Mrs. Breese (1782–
1861) is backed by a landscape that is a
virtual extension of the one in the companion portrait. Such a thorough conjunction
of paired portraits is rare.*

the "Polished Reviewer" with an attack on his undemocratic exclusivity: "Painting and its sister arts of design [take] their place in the march of civilization . . . in
the train of the *useful arts*, [which] have long and eminently occupied a distinguished place in our country." Thus the Jeffersonian principle that significant
knowledge was useful knowledge in the service of the community received another—and a notable—vote of confidence.

On the occasion of the 1828 exhibition at the National Academy of Design,
an anonymous article entitled "The Two Academies" appeared in the *Evening
Post* (May 17). Ironic—and unsubtle—it was well calculated to provoke Colonel
Trumbull:

And now turn once more to the American Academy. Look at the present exhibition. It con-

Samuel Sidney Breese

1827. Oil on wood, 16½ x 13"
Yale University Art Gallery,
New Haven, Connecticut
Gift of the Associates in Fine Arts

Morse's maternal uncle, whom he strongly resembled, Breese (1782–1861) practiced law at Cazenovia and Whitesboro in upstate New York and served in the state legislature. Beyond the deep red curtain a warmly romantic landscape is glimpsed.

tains ninety *pictures,* thirty *of which have been seen on the walls for years, (but altogether* old *and* new, *making just* half *of the number of those in the National Academy,) and these are by all manner of artists. . . . And there are* huge *copies, and* little *copies, and* whole *copies, and* half *copies, and* good *copies, and* bad *copies; indeed is a sort of Noah's Ark, in which [are] things of every kind,* clean *and* unclean, *noble animals, and* creeping things.

Unfair, certainly, but one mot that went the rounds of the art community was the answer to the question, "Have you seen the [American Academy] exhibition this year?" "No, I saw it last year."

Trumbull's bitterness and Morse's stubbornness guaranteed the continuation of the public exchange of arguments and insults into 1829. A spate of anon-

Samuel Nelson

*Nelson (1792–1873) was a judge of the
sixth circuit when painted by Morse. He
rose to become chief justice of the state Supreme Court by 1837 and associate justice
of the U.S. Supreme Court by 1845.
Morse's sympathetic portrayal is marked
by tight control of form and crisp contours.*

ymous articles did not help matters, and when Trumbull accused Morse of
authoring some of them, Morse replied heatedly:

*I pronounce [his] charge of falsehood a wanton attack on my character. I know, sir, that
Colonel Trumbull ostentatiously connects with his name associations which his countrymen
will ever cherish as sacred. But I also know, sir, that private character is a sacred thing, and
that even age, station and revolutionary associations will not shelter from public indignation
the man who assails it wantonly, especially when he himself makes an open parade of them
for the purpose.*

In the midst of this commotion, his mother, Elizabeth Ann Breese Morse,
died on May 28, 1828, only sixty-two years old. This latest blow was additionally
weighted, since it meant that Morse must find other homes for his three children,
who had been in her care since Lucretia's death.

Mrs. Samuel Nelson

1829. Oil on canvas, 31½ x 26″
New York State Historical Association,
Cooperstown

The daughter of Judge John Russell of Cooperstown, Catherine Anne Russell Nelson (1798–1875) wears a fashionable dress and a somewhat skeptical expression. She and her husband are each posed against a boldly patterned background whose designs are played against their figures with some wit.

Morse continued to visit upstate New York in the summers, and these must have been welcome breaks from the contentiousness in the city. The landscape, by turns romantic and idyllic, must have proved restorative because he began to do pure landscape paintings for the first time since England. The influence of his friend Thomas Cole, whose important landscape paintings had attracted much attention at the National Academy exhibitions, was also significant, though their attitude toward the genre differed. Morse's landscapes of 1828 were small, informal compositions, like painterly asides.

But in 1829 he painted *The View from Apple Hill*, which, while still small, stands out by virtue of its careful, classical serenity. Apple Hill was the Cooperstown estate of Judge and Mrs. Samuel Nelson from the time of their marriage in 1825 to 1829, when they sold it to General John Adams Dix. Morse had already painted the Nelsons; now he painted Mrs. Dix and her cousin, Margaret Willet,

The View from Apple Hill

WASHINGTON ALLSTON
Italian Landscape

1814. Oil on canvas, 44 x 72"
The Toledo Museum of Art, Ohio

Morse was with Allston when he painted this canvas in Bristol, England. He could not have failed to be impressed with his teacher's daring in treating landscape on such a large canvas. Since the painting seems to have remained in Bristol continuously until 1949, Morse's use of it as a model presupposes a lost drawing or other copy of it in his possession. Indeed, his return to landscape subjects for the first time since England may have called Allston's work to mind.

on the lawn of the recently transferred estate. The extensive yet domesticated view includes the foot of Otsego Lake (immortalized by James Fenimore Cooper as "Glimmerglass") at the point where the Susquehanna River emerges from it.

The fame of Cooperstown, laid out in 1788 by Fenimore's father, Judge William Cooper, owed as much to the ideals of the judge as to the novels of his son. Staying at Otsego Hall with his friend Fenimore, Morse responded to the intellectual and moral climate fostered by Judge Cooper by imbuing the cultivated hills and untroubled waters with a classical harmony. In doing so, he created one of the earliest American landscapes in which intractable nature is resolutely civilized by the hand of the painter. The assertion of human order over the wilderness is summed up, as Paul J. Staiti has eloquently expressed it, in the "thick, old tree stump that [the women] use as a rustic chair. . . . That vestigial stump of the primeval forest is now a piece of furniture in the parlor of nature, and from its ancient roots grows an ambitious pine sapling of the new, civilized order."

The companion portraits of Dr. Thomas Fuller and Mrs. Thomas Fuller, painted in June, 1829, compose a splendid coda to the five years that began with the Terry portraits and the New York triumphs. These four paintings are so quintessentially the work of Samuel F. B. Morse in pose, in technical security, in reticence and rectitude, that it is easy to overlook the subtle indications of his evolving style. The Fullers dominate their space to a greater degree and are conceived with a greater simplicity of form. At the same time they are painted with a more cursive, fluid brush that softens contours and blends colors. The colors themselves have become more various and sensuous. Whereas in his portrait of Mrs. Terry, Morse had simply played black and gray against deep red, he lends Mrs. Fuller the charm of dusty plum, pink, and blue gray, with notes of pale blue and deep rose in the face. The portraits of the Fullers bear the mark of Morse's full maturity.

The View from Apple Hill

1829. Oil on canvas, 22⅜ x 29½"
Private collection

Despite the topographical truth of the landscape as depicted by Morse, there can be little doubt that he based his composition on Washington Allston's Italian Landscape. *The high viewpoint, figure placement, arrangement of the trees to frame the scene and to skillfully link the foreground with the background are all found in the Allston. Moreover, the pacific mood, reflecting the influence of Claude Lorrain's Italian landscapes, was precisely what Morse desired for his painting.*

Mrs. Thomas Fuller

1829. Oil on canvas, 29½ x 24½"
Museum of Fine Arts, Boston

*Born in Hampton, Connecticut, Mary
Fuller (1772–1851) married Thomas
Fuller in 1793. Each portrait is inscribed
on the back, "June, 1829," together with
the sitter's age and the painter's initials.
Small preparatory oil sketches on panel for
each work are at the New York State Historical Association.*

As summer grew into fall, Morse prepared himself for his long-postponed
return to Europe. The children were delivered to relatives—Susan to the Walkers in New Hampshire, Charles and Finley to his brother Richard, now married.
And he seems to have paused to take spiritual stock of himself. The griefs and triumphs of the past five years and the crossroads at which he found himself sum-
moned up his Calvinist sense of responsibility for his life: "This life is a state of
discipline; a school in which to form character. . . . However unconscious we may
be of the fact, a thought casually conceived in the solitariness and silence and
darkness of midnight, may so modify and change the current of our future con-
duct that a blessing or a curse to millions may flow from it" (September 6).

Dr. Thomas Fuller

1829. Oil on canvas, 29½ x 24½"
Museum of Fine Arts, Boston

That there were no standards for the practice of medicine and surgery in Connecticut prior to the establishment of the Connecticut Medical Society in 1792 probably accounts for the fact that there is no record of Thomas Fuller (1765–1837) receiving a medical, or indeed any, degree. Though born in Connecticut, he began his lifelong practice in Cooperstown, New York, in 1791, was a charter member of the Otsego County Medical Society in 1806, and served the village as president of the Board of Trustees in 1818–19.

How astonishing that meditation seems to us, knowing what was to flow from Morse's thoughts on electromagnetism! But he was still a painter, about to embark on the rest of his artistic education, dedicated to his profession. On November 9, 1829, he set sail from New York on the ship *Napoleon*, armed with the good wishes of his friends and colleagues and, more importantly, a list of commissions from them that would underwrite his tour.

VII. "Exertions and Sacrifices"

HORATIO GREENOUGH (1805–1852)
Samuel F. B. Morse

1831. Marble, 19½ x 12 x 8¾"
National Museum of American Art,
Washington, D.C.

From Florence, Morse wrote to John Lud-
low Morton (April 18, 1831): "Mr.
Greenough has just completed a bust of
me, which all say is an excellent likeness.
He insisted on my fulfilling my promise to
him in New York of sitting to him for my
bust. It may be in New York in season for
the [National Academy] exhibition of
1832." In fact it was not exhibited there
until 1833.

FIRED WITH ENTHUSIASM TO RAISE THE LEVEL of artistic taste in America, Morse had sailed home from England fourteen years earlier. Now, distinguished as founder and president of the National Academy of Design, he arrived in Liverpool on December 4, 1829, after a twenty-six-day crossing. He went on to London with some speed, for he intended to spend less than a fortnight before crossing the Channel to France.

There can be no doubt that the overriding purpose of Morse's extended sojourn in Europe was to prepare himself for the execution of a painting in the Capitol Rotunda, a commission he fully expected. We may assume that he shared this ambition with many of his friends, and that at least some of the subscribers to his trip knew of its purpose. William Cullen Bryant did. At the end of December, 1828, he had written to Gulian Verplanck, chairman of the Congressional Committee on Public Buildings, recommending artists for the four commissions, especially Morse, "who is going abroad next spring—to Rome—who will study it there, and give five years of his life to it."

Morse's U.S. passport bears implicit witness to his intentions and renewed pride in his profession, for he is described as "Historical Painter and President of the National Academy of Design." That "historical painting" had played little part in a twenty-year career could be ignored in the certainty that it would now become central.

The nearly three years Morse spent in Europe this time were crammed with incident and new experiences, but of the many copies and original works painted then relatively few are known today. In London, he first went to see Charles Robert Leslie, his roommate from Royal Academy days, and together they toured the city, visited Washington Irving, went to the newly founded National Gallery, and called on J. M. W. Turner ("the best landscape painter living"). He left London for the port of Dover on December 22, accompanied by Americans—the artist Nathaniel Jocelyn and the architect Ithiel Town. En route he was greatly impressed by the architecture of Canterbury Cathedral and by the emotional grandeur of the music of the service, but the High Church liturgy discomfited him—"I say nothing of devotion."

Although the Channel crossing was delayed until December 29, on January 1, 1830, Samuel Morse, aged thirty-eight, entered Paris at last. He went immediately to the Louvre, where he "buried himself" among the 1,250 paintings then hanging in the Grand Gallery. "Here I have marked out several which I shall

118

copy on my return from Italy." During this first brief stay in Paris, he was cordially received by the Marquis de Lafayette, continuing the friendship that had begun in Washington and New York. Morse had intended to write an occasional series of articles in the form of "letters" for the *Journal of Commerce*. Now he had second thoughts: "I find my pen and pencil are enemies to each other. I must write less and paint more" (January 7).

On January 13 the three friends left Paris on the journey to Italy. They sketched the landscape and the people, and Morse kept a journal in which his complex response to Catholicism is often recorded. Although sensually attracted to the majestic architecture and the pageantry, especially the music, his Calvinist nature rebelled against these distractions from devotion. It was a fundamental conflict—the artist as iconoclast—and incapable of resolution.

After a mass at Avignon, he commented: "Far be it from me to say there were not some who were actually devout, hard as it is to conceive of such a thing. . . . The imagination was addressed by every avenue. . . . No instruction was imparted." That is the didactic, moral voice of Samuel Morse, which is also found in his scant handful of history paintings—paintings in which "instruction was imparted" while the "charms of mere sense" were given less attention.

They reached Nice (then Italian) by the end of the month. Now they adopted a more leisurely pace, and Morse found much to delight him in Lombardy and Tuscany. He had a romantic response to the Apennine landscape ("stupendous mountains" and "brawling cascades"), which he saw with a painter's eye: "Long slopes of clay color were interlocked with dark browns sprinkled with golden yellow; slate blue and grey, mixed with greens and purples, and the pure, deep ultramarine blue of distant peaks finished the background." After brief stops in Lucca, Pisa, and Florence, on February 20 Morse entered Rome at Porta del Popolo and soon found a room at No. 17, Via dei Prefetti, between the Corso and the Tiber, not far from the Piazza Navona.

Finally he could unpack his bags in anticipation of a long stay and begin to paint again. For more than two months his work had been mostly restricted to sketches made on the wing as his tour unfolded. Now he began to attend to the list of commissions from the twenty New York patrons whose cash advances totaling more than three thousand dollars were underwriting his adventure. The list called for at least twenty-eight paintings, including copies and original works. On March 7 he wrote: "I have begun to copy the 'School of Athens' from Raphael for Mr. R. [Robert] Donaldson." For this copy, which he estimated would take five or six weeks, he had been paid one hundred dollars. While copying the Old Masters was part of Morse's continuing "education," it was clear that he would be earning his passage.

Although Paris was rising to preeminence among European art capitals, Rome had its incomparable monuments and an extensive international community of artists, amateurs, and literati. Most European nationalities were represented, but Germans from Prussia and Bavaria were the largest group, as they had been for decades. Closely associated with the Germans was the Dane Bertel Thorvaldsen, regarded as the greatest living sculptor.

Bertel Thorvaldsen

1830–31. Oil on canvas, 30 x 25"
His Majesty the King of Denmark

"He is an old man in appearance having a profusion of grey hair, wildly hanging over his forehead and ears. His face has a strong Northern character, his eyes are light grey, and his complexion sandy; he is a large man of perfectly unassuming manners and . . . without the least appearance of ostentation." The portrait of Thorvaldsen (1770–1844) was shipped to Philip Hone, whose hundred-dollar subscription to Morse's trip was for a subject of the artist's choice. Thirty-seven years later the painting was returned to Morse by John Taylor Johnston, a great collector and the first president of the Metropolitan Museum of Art, so that the artist could present it to the King of Denmark in memory of Thorvaldsen.

Chapel of the Virgin at Subiaco

Study for *Chapel of the Virgin at Subiaco*

1830. Oil on paper mounted on canvas,
8¾ x 10¾"
Worcester Art Museum, Massachusetts

The large finished landscape was delivered to Stephen Salisbury II in return for the two hundred dollars Salisbury had subscribed to Morse's fund. This small study was given to another patron, J. L. Morton, who for his thirty dollars had requested a Madonna. Painted on the spot, unlike the large canvas, it is utterly naturalistic in light and color and in the observation of foliage and architecture. Perhaps the breadth of the scene attracted Morse, who conveys the space logically and convincingly.

Morse and Thorvaldsen were introduced at a soiree on April 16, and the latter "readily assented . . . to sit for his portrait which I hope soon to take." The sittings did not take place until the fall of the year, and the portrait was probably not completed before early 1831.

In the late spring and early summer of 1830 Morse twice went out of the city with other artists to explore and sketch in the cooler environs of Rome—Tivoli and Subiaco, Albano, Ariccia, and Genzano. Of his trip to Subiaco, he wrote:

I stopped . . . to look around and down into the chasm below. It was enchanting in spite of the atmosphere of the sirocco. The hills covered with woods, at a distance, reminded me of my own country, fresh and variegated; the high peaks beyond were grey from distance, and the sides of the nearer mountains were marked with many a winding track, down one of which a shepherd and his sheep were descending, looking like a moving pathway. No noise disturbed the silence but the distant barking of the shepherd's dog . . . mixing with the faint murmuring of the waterfall and the song of the birds that inhabited the ilex grove. It was altogether a place suited to meditation, and, were it consistent with those duties which man owes his fellow man, here would be the spot to which one, fond of study and averse to the noise and bustle of the world, would love to retire.

It is a remarkably idyllic passage, redolent of place, even though qualified by the low whisper of "duty." The peaceful silence evoked by Morse's words is elevated to a poetic level in his *Chapel of the Virgin at Subiaco*. The landscape crowned by the monastery of San Benedetto at Subiaco was the inspiration for a fascinating painting that combines stylistic elements from Allston's beloved Venetian painters and the German artists resident in Rome. Using the luminous glazes

Chapel of the Virgin at Subiaco

1830. Oil on canvas, 29⅞ x 37"
Worcester Art Museum, Massachusetts

In this painting Morse seems in accord with the view soon to be expressed by Ralph Waldo Emerson that "in landscapes the painter should give the suggestion of a fairer creation than we know. The details, the prose of nature he should omit and give us only the spirit and splendor. He should know that the landscape has beauty for his eye because it expresses a thought which is to him good." This is an idea found in art as early as the neoplatonic writers of the sixteenth century, but it became a particularly consistent attitude toward landscape among American painters and writers.

that he had learned about from Allston, Morse re-creates the atmosphere of early morning's rising mist, but his idiosyncratic, unnaturalistic palette idealizes the effect in a Keatsian vein: "Was it a vision, or a waking dream?"

The few but prominent figures in the landscape, on the other hand, speak a different language. In their crisp, silhouetted elegance they are similar to figures in the paintings of Josef Anton Koch and other German artists who had been active in Rome for some years. Together with the strong contrast of dark foreground against bright background, these figures suggest an operatic tableau.

Morse described the chapel, which is the central focus of the painting, in a letter: "This chapel stands by the side of the road upon a hill east of Subiaco, and is a good example of those shrines before which the contadini bow the knee, and worship the virgin; in the distance is the town of Subiaco." In another painting he excluded the chapel and depicted only the *Contadina at the Shrine of the Madonna.* Morse's aversion to the "idolatry of the Virgin Mary" precluded a successful evocation of piety. But he did effectively combine the picturesque with the serenity that marked the large landscape, and he was careful to avoid the sentimental genre image so common in the nineteenth century.

When not in the countryside, Morse spent long hours studying and copying in the Vatican and the Palazzo Colonna, fulfilling commissions while absorbing the varied art to be seen there. Despite the intense summer heat, he traveled farther south in July, accompanied by four friends. They arrived in Naples on July 11, where they remained, with side trips to Sorrento, Amalfi, and Capri, until early September. At the end of November the moderately liberal Pope Pius VIII died, to be succeeded in February, 1831, by the reactionary Gregory XVI. Rumors of revolution had circulated in December, and on February 10 Morse noted in his journal: "The revolutions in the Papal States to the north at Bologna and Ancona, and in the Duchy of Modena, have been made known at Rome. Great consternation prevails." The political tension was unsettling to the foreign community in Rome, especially to artists, who were assumed to be liberals.

On March 4, 1831, Morse prudently left Rome for Florence. Inspired by the July Revolution of 1830 in Paris, the scattered insurrections of early 1831 were uncoordinated and minor in the long view of history. But to an American then in Rome they must have seemed ominous. Indeed, although the revolts were suppressed with Austrian aid, in that same month Giuseppe Mazzini founded Young Italy, the revolutionary society that led directly to the Italian war of independence of 1848–49. Once again, as in London during the War of 1812, Morse found himself a witness to a crucial moment of contemporary history.

Arriving in Florence on March 9, he soon went to the Uffizi Gallery, where he copied, among other works, self-portraits by Rubens and Titian for another New York patron, Martin Van Schaick. After two months in the city, he traveled via Bologna and Ferrara to Venice, where he passed two more months. At the Accademia during a violent thunderstorm, "the rain penetrated through the ceiling at the corner of the picture I was copying—'The Miracle of the Slave,' by Tintoret—and threatened injury to it, but happily it escaped." This copy had

Contadina at the Shrine of the Madonna

1830. Oil on canvas, 21½ x 17¼"
Virginia Museum of Fine Arts, Richmond

Another of Morse's patrons, Charles Carvill, had requested something small, "like Leslie's Ann Page*" (which belonged to Philip Hone). For his hundred dollars he received the* Contadina.

The Wetterhorn and Falls of the Reichenbach

c. 1831–32. Oil on canvas, 23 x 16⅛"
Collection of the Newark Museum, New Jersey
Bequest of Dr. J. Ackerman Coles, 1926

Instead of transcendental grandeur, this tall but small landscape evokes the tranquillity of the sparsely settled valleys of the Alps, where the daily pastoral existence ignores the awesome peaks. Although influenced by the similar landscapes of the German painter Josef Anton Koch, Morse rejects his spatial sweep for intimacy. The Alpine wildness affected him, but the civilizing instinct was very strong in Morse.

The Wetterhorn and Falls of the Reichenbach

been specified by his brother-in-law, Charles Walker, who paid five hundred dollars for it, by far the most generous subscription.

On July 18 he left Venice and crossed northern Italy to Milan. There, after witnessing the service in the cathedral ("a most gorgeous building, far exceeding my conception of it"), he again pondered this, to him, alien faith:

> *It is a religion of the imagination. . . . architecture, painting, sculpture, music, have lent all their charm to enchant the senses and impose on the understanding by substituting for the solemn truths of God's Word, which are addressed to the understanding, the fictions of poetry and the delusions of feeling. . . . I have been led, since I have been in Italy, to think much of the propriety of introducing pictures into churches in aid of devotion. I have certainly every inducement to decide in favor of the practice. . . . That pictures may and do have the effect upon some rightly to raise the affections, I have no doubt . . . but, knowing that man is led astray by his imagination more than by any of his other faculties . . . I had rather sacrifice the interests of the arts . . . than run the risk.*

The man who would be a historical painter had consciously and definitively ruled out probably the largest single category of history paintings—religious—despite the fact that his mentors, Benjamin West and Washington Allston, also non-Catholics, had willingly embraced it.

Leaving Italy by way of Lake Como and Lake Maggiore in early August, Morse crossed the Alps for Switzerland. The Alpine landscape, with its intimations of divine creation, stirred him deeply. Though unable to attend church one Sunday, "I have yet on the top of this mountain a place of private worship such as I have not had for some time past. I am alone on the mountain with such a scene spread before me that I must adore. . . . [Faith lifts] the heart from nature up to nature's God." From sketches made in the Alps, Morse later painted at least one landscape, *The Wetterhorn and Falls of the Reichenbach*, which he presented to Jonathan Goodhue, another subscriber.

It was a much-altered Paris that Morse entered on September 12, 1831. The July Revolution had traded a Bourbon monarch, Charles X, for a bourgeois monarch, Louis Philippe. The Marquis de Lafayette was once again a man of great influence in France. Early in 1832 the horrific pandemic of cholera that had begun in India in 1826 reached France (it spread then to North America, lingering until 1838). In Paris, Morse reported on May 6, as many as "fifteen hundred [persons] were seized in a day, and fifteen thousand at least have already perished, although the official accounts will not give so many."

Despite the extreme risk to his health, Morse worked unceasingly on an elaborate project that he had begun late in the fall—a painting of the *Gallery of the Louvre* on the largest canvas he had prepared since *The House of Representatives*. The gallery in question was the Salon Carré, from which the name "Salon" was given to the annual exhibitions of the Royal Academy of Painting and Sculpture held there, and in which, now that it was a public museum, selected masterpieces of European painting and sculpture in the French national collection—some of them Napoleonic plunder—were displayed. Or rather, in which they had been displayed up to 1830, when Morse first saw the room. Probably because of the

Gallery of the Louvre

1831–33. Oil on canvas, 73¾ x 108"
Collection Terra Museum of American Art,
Chicago, Illinois

Although the golden tonality of the painting suggests the varnishes of Old Master paintings themselves, one glance at the oil study of Titian's Francis I *dispels any notion that this was calculated. The pure, unmuddied colors of the study must surely have been copied onto the large canvas, which, if cleaned, might still reveal a similar brilliance and range. The light flowing through the gallery is skillfully distributed and controlled, especially in the half-lights. Morse has inscribed his initials and the date 1833 on the back of a small canvas leaning against the wall behind the miniature painter.*

nationalist pretensions of the new regime, the gallery had been rededicated exclusively to the French school, as may be seen in engravings and paintings of the period.

Morse was not excessively fond of French painting and actively disliked modern French painting, such as Géricault's 1819 *Raft of the Medusa,* which now dominated the Salon Carré. So the American artist simply used his imagination to rehang the gallery in its former manner or, more accurately, with his own choices from the Louvre's riches. It is this "musée imaginaire" that he would in two years' time exhibit to the American public.

Morse's purpose in painting the picture is a much-examined topic. The usual conclusion is that he wished to introduce into America, if only in copies, some of the greatest European art, not as mere curiosities but in order to edify his countrymen—artists, collectors, and the refined public alike—in matters of taste. But similar copies were already widely known in the United States. Some were purchased in Europe by American travelers. Others had been commissioned from native artists such as John Vanderlyn, who had painted copies of great works by Titian, Veronese, Correggio, Caravaggio, and Rubens, most of which were exhibited at the American Academy of the Fine Arts nearly thirty years before Morse finished his gallery picture. Morse himself, of course, was continuing this tradition with his subscription copies in Europe.

Although he certainly expected his *Gallery* to be admired for the paintings therein, it also seems likely that he was consciously continuing his preparation for the expected Rotunda commission. This he could do by absorbing the art of painters who had frequently worked on large decorative murals, from Raphael, Titian, and Veronese to Rubens and Reni. In this he believed himself successful: "I have many compliments on it, and I am sure it is the most *correct* one of *its kind* ever painted, for everyone says I have caught the style of each of the masters."

It is logical to assume that his selection of Old Masters represented his personal taste. Certainly the seven Venetian paintings and at least ten paintings reflecting Venetian influence bear witness—in their placement no less than their numbers—to the admiration for that school instilled in Morse by Allston. But there are less obvious inclusions, such as the Jouvenet *Deposition* hanging next to the Veronese at the left, or even the several Murillos. Murillo was immensely popular, but his subject matter, alternating between supersaturated religious themes and sentimental genre, was far from Morse's historical ideal. The reasons behind his choices still deserve much study.

The prototypes for such gallery pictures go back to the seventeenth century. Some of them were essentially inventories of private or royal collections, such as those painted by David Teniers for the Archduke Leopold Wilhelm of the Netherlands. Others, particularly in the eighteenth century, were imaginary collections, especially of famous sculpture of antiquity and supposed paintings of ancient monuments. Of much greater interest for Morse's composition is an exactly contemporary work by the little-known English painter John Scarlett Davis, *Main Gallery of the Louvre, Paris,* in which the viewpoint is nearly the same and which includes (out of a smaller total) seven of the same paintings, five of them

JOHN SCARLETT DAVIS
Main Gallery of the Louvre, Paris

1831. Oil on canvas, 46 x 57½"
Courtesy of The Fine Arts Society Ltd.,
London, England

Davis painted other museum interiors. Although a far more prosaic record than Morse's ideal painting, it is hard to avoid the conclusion that Davis's version inspired the American in many details and perhaps even in the initial conception.

Detail of *Gallery of the Louvre*

The animated Cooper family is placed near Rembrandt's The Angel Leaving Tobias *(next to the door), a copy of which they had commissioned from Morse. The woman and child in Breton costume represent the new, nonaristocratic public for art; their taut purity of shape makes a nice contrast with the full, flowing forms in the Murillo* Holy Family, *to which the woman's tall headdress points. The brightest area in the painting is the view into the Grand Gallery framed by the door, where Morse conjures an aura both opulent and inviting. As the largest figures, centrally placed, Morse and his student are a strong focal point. She is drawing the head of a bearded, turbaned old man, certainly from one of the figures in the Veronese that she faces.*

hanging in the same or nearly the same positions. The latter circumstance probably reflects the actual disposition of the paintings in the Salon Carré prior to 1831. Since Davis's painting is dated 1831, it may be a literal record of the gallery before the rehanging; compared to the Morse, it is quite casual and unstructured. But Davis's picture may possibly have served as the source of inspiration for Morse's more fanciful and personal reconstruction. It is also worth recalling that Morse had recently copied Raphael's *School of Athens,* whose spatial configuration—a brightly lit foreground space with figures and a long, vaulted gallery alternately dark and bright stretching beyond—is markedly similar to Morse's plan.

Morse's working method on the *Gallery of the Louvre* paralleled that on his *House of Representatives.* He took the full canvas into the Louvre and recorded the architectural setting, with its double focus on the salon and on the vista of the Grand Gallery beyond. Concurrently he made small copies of all of the paintings to be included, probably with the help of a camera obscura. In his studio he copied them onto the large canvas, frequently changing their relative sizes to accommodate his compositional aims. Later, back in America, he added their frames; and lastly he introduced the figures, ten in the Salon Carré itself and an indeterminate number of tiny figures in the Grand Gallery beyond.

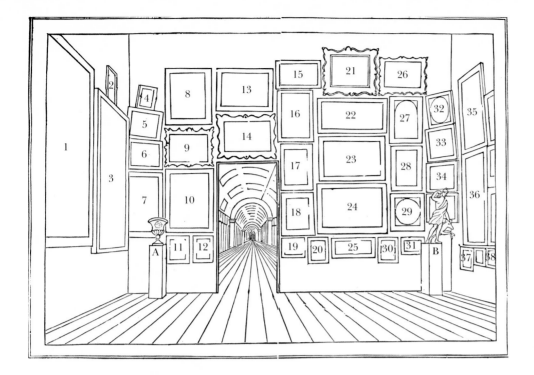

Morse's Key to the Pictures

1833. Engraving, 5¼ x 7¾"
The New-York Historical Society, New York

This key was published in Morse's De-scriptive Catalogue *for the exhibition of the painting. The numbers he used were the inventory numbers then in use at the Louvre. They have been replaced with consecutive numbers from 1 to 38, and the sculpture has also been identified. Titles have been changed where necessary to conform to standard usage. Morse omitted all the figures from his key; he may have been reluctant to identify himself and Cooper publicly after receipt of the latter's letter quoted in the text.*

1. Veronese, *The Marriage of Cana*
2. Murillo, *Immaculate Conception*
3. Jouvenet, *The Descent from the Cross*
4. Tintoretto, *Self-Portrait*
5. Poussin, *Winter (The Deluge)*
6. Caravaggio, *The Fortune Teller*
7. Titian, *Christ Crowned with Thorns*
8. Van Dyck, *Venus Entreating Vulcan*
9. Claude Lorrain, *The Disembarkation of Cleopatra at Tarsus*
10. Murillo, *The Holy Family*
11. Teniers the Younger, *The Knife Grinder*
12. Rembrandt, *The Angel Leaving Tobias and his Family*
13. Poussin, *Diogenes Casting Away His Cup*
14. Titian, *Supper at Emmaus*
15. Huysmans, *Landscape*
16. Van Dyck, *Portrait of a Lady and Her Daughter*
17. Titian, *Francis I*
18. Murillo, *The Young Beggar*
19. Veronese, *Christ Fallen Under the Cross*
20. Leonardo da Vinci, *Mona Lisa*
21. Correggio, *Mystic Marriage of St. Catherine*
22. Rubens, *The Flight of Lot and His Family from Sodom*
23. Claude Lorrain, *Seaport, with Setting Sun*
24. Titian, *Entombment*
25. Le Sueur, *Christ Bearing the Cross*
26. Salvator Rosa, *Landscape with Soldiers and Hunters*
27. Raphael, *"La Belle Jardinière" (Madonna and Child with St. John)*
28. Van Dyck, *Man Dressed in Black*
29. Guido Reni, *The Union of Design and Color*
30. Rubens, *Susanna Fourment*
31. Cantarini, *Rest on the Flight to Egypt*
32. Rembrandt, *Portrait of an Old Man*
33. Van Dyck, *The Woman Taken in Adultery*
34. Joseph Vernet, *A Marine View by Moonlight*
35. Guido Reni, *Nessus and Dejanira*
36. Rubens, *Queen Tomyris with the Head of Cyrus*
37. Mignard, *The Virgin of the Grapes*
38. Watteau, *Embarkation from Cythera*

A. Perhaps *The Borghese Vase*, Neo-Attic, Athenian
B. *"Diane Chasseresse"*, Roman copy of Greek original

The foreground figures include his good friend James Fenimore Cooper, whom he seems to have first met in Washington at President Monroe's soiree on February 9, 1824: "I went last night in a carriage with . . . Mr. Cooper, the celebrated author of the popular American novels." He continued the friendship in New York and in Cooperstown before departing for Europe. The Cooper family was in Rome in 1830, where Morse "passed many pleasant hours with them, particularly one beautiful moonlight evening visiting the Coliseum." The Coopers preceded him to Paris, where they and Morse became inseparable. While Morse worked on his large canvas and the small copies, Cooper haunted the Louvre, commenting in his blunt, irrepressible way: "Lay it on here, Samuel . . . more yellow—the nose is too short—the eye too small—damn it, if I had been a painter what a picture I should have painted."

The identifiable figures in the *Gallery of the Louvre* are Cooper, his wife, and his daughter (seated, with palette in hand) in the back left corner and Morse instructing a student (who might possibly be his daughter, Susan, since the figures were added in New York) front and center.

Morse hung "his" gallery with great care, and almost certainly with didactic intent. It rewards close study. While there are many intriguing placements and juxtapositions of paintings, none is more interesting than that of Titian's *Francis I*, virtually in the center of the canvas and above Morse. That the Titian has been made relatively much larger than it is and that the purity of Morse's profile parallels that of Francis suggests that the artist had a point to make.

Since American patronage was one of Morse's central concerns, the central position of Francis I—one of the great Renaissance art patrons—may be a reproof to contemporary patrons. The *Mona Lisa*, which hangs below *Francis I* and behind Morse, entered the royal collections through the patronage of Francis I, whose friendship with Leonardo da Vinci was the stuff of artistic legend. (Apropos, Ingres's first version of *The Death of Leonardo da Vinci* in the arms of Francis I was painted in 1818.) At the same time, that the American is depicted facing in the opposite direction from Francis may be wittily intended, as Cooper had said of one of his books, to suggest "how differently a democrat and an aristocrat saw the same thing." It has often been observed that Morse's painting was the first gallery picture from which aristocrats had been excluded. Middle class and casual, the artists and visitors in the *Gallery of the Louvre* are the legitimate democratic heirs of the great tradition of aristocratic art.

Cooper's connection with Morse and with this painting had several additional aspects. First, it is thought that Morse may have made an offer of marriage to Susan Fenimore Cooper, the eldest daughter, to whom he was giving art lessons. Second, speaking of the large painting in a letter to his brothers (July 18, 1832), Morse wrote, "Cooper is delighted with it and I think he will own it," though what guarantees Cooper had made are unknown. And finally, sometime after Morse's return to America in mid-November, Cooper, who had recently been much criticized in the American press, wrote him a cautionary letter concerning the exhibition of the *Gallery*: "I doubt your success in New York, and would advise you to try Philadelphia. Your intimacy with me has become known, and such is the virulence of my enemies in New York that I have no sort of doubt of their attacking your picture in consequence."

In the letter to his brothers quoted above, Morse spoke at length of his assessment of and affection for Cooper:

He has a bold, original, independent mind, thoroughly American. He loves his country and her principles most ardently. . . . He never asks what effect any of his sentiments will have upon the sale of his works; the only question he asks is—'Are they just and true?' . . . He is not a religious man (I wish from my heart he was), yet he is . . . a great respecter of religion and religious men, a man of unblemished moral character. . . . He never compromises the dignity of an American citizen, which he contends is the highest distinction a man can have in Europe. . . . I admire exceedingly his proud assertion of the rank of an American.

Obviously, aside from the delicate matter of religion, Morse identified himself with Cooper's beliefs and envied his unguarded exuberance.

In September he paid his parting respects to Lafayette, crossed the Channel for a farewell visit with Leslie, and returned to Le Havre, from which he sailed for America in early October, debarking in New York on November 15, 1832. The voyage on the *Sully* was momentous, not for the history of art but for the history of technology. It was during this passage, in the course of conversation on electricity and electromagnetism, that Morse conceived the idea of the electric telegraph: "I see no reason why intelligence might not be instantaneously transmitted by electricity to any distance."

On arrival, full of fervor, he soon began trying to fabricate the various mechanical devices that would permit the electric circuit to be opened and closed, so that a signal could be sent, and make possible the recording of the received message. In addition, he was soon overwhelmed by the business of the National Academy of Design, which had missed his leadership. The *Gallery of the Louvre*

Francis I

c. 1831–32. Oil on panel, 10 x 8"
Gift of Berry-Hill Galleries
Collection Terra Museum of American Art,
Chicago, Illinois

There is a tracing of this figure, of the same size, at the National Academy of Design, which reveals Morse's working method. It is in reverse, so it must have been made with the aid of the camera obscura, which commonly projects the reversed image onto the paper. After the design was transferred to the small panel, the painting of the copy would have proceeded. This excellently preserved study supports Morse's claim that "everyone says I have caught the style of each of the masters." On the back is inscribed: "To C. R. Leslie RA from his old friend SFBM./NY Apr. 1834." Leslie had arrived in New York in November, 1833, to accept an appointment as professor of drawing at West Point but returned to London in 1834.

Francis I

Mrs. Jacob (Catharine Ludlow) Morton

1833. Oil on canvas, 30 x 25"
The New-York Historical Society, New York

Morse knew Mrs. Morton (1767–1849) and her husband, Jacob, through their artist-son, John Ludlow Morton, who was the first secretary of the National Academy of Design. In addition to this portrait, Morse graciously agreed to copy, as a pendant, a portrait of Jacob Morton painted by Morse's younger rival, Henry Inman. The present work is inscribed on the back: "painted by SFB Morse, Esqr PNA for JLM 1833."

was put aside until February, 1833. His depleted finances prodded him to renew work on the painting, on which so much effort had been expended and so many hopes pinned. Finally, on August 9 he wrote to Cooper, "My picture *c'est fini.*"

When it was exhibited in the fall, it received a glowing review in the New York *Mirror*:

[We know] not which most to admire in contemplating this magnificent design, the courage which could undertake such a Herculean task, or the perseverance and success with which it has been completed. We have never seen anything of the kind before in this country. . . . This representation of the Louvre . . . grows in interest at every fresh view, and we have found ourselves unconsciously lingering for hours, and yet have been unable to exhaust its beauties.

EXERTIONS AND SACRIFICES

Dr. William Buell Sprague

1834. Oil on wood, 10 x 8″
Slater Memorial Museum, Norwich Free Academy,
Norwich, Connecticut

*This tiny painting is inscribed on the back:
"painted and presented to/Rev. Dr.
Sprague/by Samuel FB Morse/New York/
June 20, 1834." It was not a commission
but painted without charge as a model for
an engraving by Asher B. Durand.
Sprague (1795–1876), for forty years
pastor of the Second Presbyterian Church
in Albany, returned the favor handsomely
thirty years later when he wrote* The Life
of Jedidiah Morse, D.D., *with the cooperation of his sons.*

Unhappily, William Dunlap observed, although "Every artist and connoisseur
was charmed with it . . . it was 'caviare to the multitude.' Those who had flocked
to see the nudity of Adam and Eve, had no curiosity to see this beautiful and cu-
rious specimen of art." And so the exhibition failed in its immediate aim—to earn
money for its author—as *The House of Representatives* had failed eleven years before. In desperation he took it to New Haven, where it had even less public
success.

As the year ended, he wrote:

*I have had for three weeks more hopeless despondence in regard to the future, than I have
ever before suffered. . . . [I must] try to live if I can; to last through life, to stifle all aspiring*

George Hyde Clarke

thoughts after an excellence in art, about which I can only dream, an excellence which I see and felt I might attain, but which for 20 years has been within sight but never within grasp. My life of poetry and romance is gone.

The following August he sold the painting to George Hyde Clarke of Otsego for thirteen hundred dollars (with the frame, and on credit!), although he had earlier expected it would bring twenty-five hundred dollars. When he suggested to Clarke that he add the figure of the recently deceased Lafayette to the foreground, he discovered that his tightfisted patron was mean-spirited as well. The exceedingly conservative Clarke defamed Morse's friend as "a utopian, a philosopher that only comprehended half of liberty."

In his letter to Clarke, Morse added: "I have lately changed my plans in relation to this picture and to my art generally. . . . I have need of funds to prosecute my new plans." His change of plans was known to others. His great friend the sculptor Horatio Greenough wrote from Italy: "I am grieved to hear that you have decided on confining yourself to portrait." It was more than that, of course. He turned his attention from painting to the development of his idea for the telegraph, which would eventually absorb all his time and energy.

In the same vein, he attended closely to the health of the National Academy of Design, for he was "more and more persuaded that I have quite as much to do with the pen for the arts as the pencil, and if I can in my day so enlighten the public as to make the way easier for those that come after me, I don't know that I shall not have served the cause of fine arts as effectively as by painting pictures which might be appreciated one hundred years after I am gone" (February 21, 1833).

The pivotal year 1834 also marked Morse's plunge into politics as a polemical writer. His theme was the basic hostility to democratic freedoms that he ascribed to Catholicism. His pulpit was the religious press in the United States, including his brothers' paper. His anti-Catholic, antiforeign rhetoric first burbled into print in the *New-York Observer* in a series of articles republished as *Foreign Conspiracy against the Liberties of the United States* (1835). This was followed by *Imminent Dangers* (1835), an anti-immigrant pamphlet, and *Confessions of a French Catholic Priest* (1837), which Morse edited.

In these vitriolic tracts he was not guided by dislike of the Catholic liturgical practices that had so preoccupied him in Europe. Rather, it was Catholicism as a political institution that he raged against. He had seen the antirepublican sentiments that characterized the church hierarchy during the postrevolutionary period, and he had been profoundly influenced by Lafayette, who, although Catholic, was staunchly opposed to any church involvement in political life. But Morse's nativism grew so shrill that we must wonder if the timing of these outbursts was not subconsciously tied to his professional crisis as an artist.

In 1836 he was persuaded to run for mayor of New York City on the Native American ticket, after Philip Hone declined the nomination. His principles would not permit him to renounce his Democratic allegiance, however, and so the Whig party, natural allies of the Nativists against the Democrats, nominated their own candidate and split the vote. Fenimore Cooper wrote bemusedly to

George Hyde Clarke

1829. Oil on canvas, 43⅛ x 34¾"
The Saint Louis Art Museum, Missouri

Painted five years before Clarke (1768–1835) acquired the Gallery of the Louvre, *the portrait captures the imperious demeanor of this hereditary landowner. In the background is Hyde Hall, the country house on Otsego Lake built for Clarke by Philip Hooker, architect of the capitol building in Albany. The view is of the veranda, "looking like a Jamaican overseer's house" and reminding us of the family's sugar plantations on that island—the source of much of Clarke's wealth. His consort (no marriage has been established) was the widow of Fenimore Cooper's brother, and it may have been Cooper who suggested that he purchase the* Gallery *when the novelist felt unable to do so.*

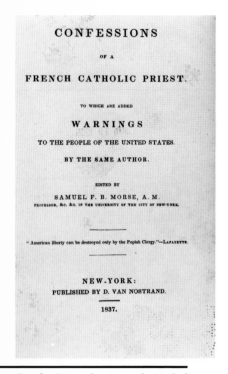

Confessions of a French Catholic Priest

First printed in 1837.
Dartmouth College Library,
Hanover, New Hampshire

This manuscript was edited by Morse, who refused to identify the priest who presented it to him in order to safeguard the priest's relatives in France. It was not primarily a political tract but a scandal sheet that purported to describe the immoral and luxurious lives of the Catholic clergy and monastic communities.

Greenough: "What do you think of Morse for a Mayor? The fellow actually got 1,800 votes for that grave and masticating office . . . and would have been elected had he got 18,000 more."

As if this burst of public activity were not sufficient, Morse had accepted a nondutied, nonsalaried appointment to the faculty of New York University, apparently shortly after his return in 1832. When the university building was finished in 1835, Morse rented the top room in the northwest tower of the neo-Gothic structure and a suite of five rooms for his residence on the floor below. He was professor of the literature of the arts of design, and any students he brought in would pay tuition directly to him.

The didactic, idealistic side of Morse was at ease in this new setting, and his *Allegorical Landscape with New York University* is the expression of an intellectual rather than a romantic visionary. The original title was more specific: *Landscape Composition, Helicon and Aganippe*. The Muses, divinities presiding over the arts and sciences, lived on Mount Helicon with Apollo, the Greek embodiment of civilization. The spring, Aganippe, flows from Helicon into the serene lagoon, on the other shore of which is the New York University building. A statue of Athena, goddess of wisdom and protectress of Athenian democracy, mediates between the classic past and the democratic present at the juncture of a bridge on the road between them. The rising sun illuminates the university, announcing the passage of the European intellectual tradition to the New World. Although couched in traditional allegorical terms, the message is the same as that of the *Gallery of the Louvre*, now extended from art to all knowledge.

Apart from his teaching, Morse's studio became the center of his telegraphic investigations. A colleague at New York University, Leonard D. Gale, professor of geology and mineralogy, saw Morse's rudimentary telegraphic setup at the beginning of 1836. Recognizing that Morse's battery and magnet were too weak, he helped him develop a multicelled battery and a multiloop magnet. In September, 1837, he became an official partner in Morse's enterprise.

The paintings between 1833 and 1837 were often of a very high order, but they were mostly of a personal kind, such as portraits of family and friends and the *Allegorical Landscape*. But for much of that period Morse still had high hopes for the public commission that would redeem the failure of his previous history paintings and vindicate his artistic ideals—the Capitol Rotunda painting for which he and his friends had lobbied for years. With such strategically placed friends in government as Gulian Verplanck, whose position on the Buildings Committee that oversaw projects in the Capitol boded well for his artist friend, Morse had every expectation of success.

Precisely what went awry has never been established. Probably it was a combination of factors. Arguments in Congress over the relative merits of American and European artists prevented a bill introduced in January, 1834, from being considered that year. In 1836 a Joint Resolution "to contract with one or more American artists" to fill the four remaining commissions passed easily. In committee it was agreed that Washington Allston, the dean of American artists,

Allegorical Landscape with New York University

1835–36. Oil on canvas, 22 x 36"
The New-York Historical Society, New York

The English Collegiate Gothic style of Alexander Jackson Davis's university building included a central chapel with a huge tracery window derived from King's College Chapel, Cambridge. In the implicit Christian reference carried by the architecture, Morse's painting contrasts with the exactly contemporary Consummation of Empire *by his friend Thomas Cole, which in certain other respects probably served as a model. Morse's palette is very close to his Subiaco landscape, while his composition, as Paul J. Staiti has astutely observed, "is the* House of Representatives *transplanted outside."*

The Goldfish Bowl

JOHN VANDERLYN (1775–1852)
Niagara Falls from Table Rock

c. 1801–2. Oil on canvas, 24 x 30″
Museum of Fine Arts, Boston

On the back is inscribed: "To Nath. Jocelyn./Sam. F. B. Morse/New Haven— 1835." As a result, the painting had been ascribed to Morse and for decades reproduced as such in publications, until its reattribution in 1975. Since it repeats the composition of an 1804 engraving after Vanderlyn, it was assumed that Morse copied the engraving. Stylistically this is untenable, as a comparison with the Allegorical Landscape *makes clear. The painting must therefore be Vanderlyn's original, which served as model for the engraving. The words on the back are simply a gift inscription, although it is not known when Morse acquired the painting.*

should be offered two. Entangled in his ill-fated *Belshazzar's Feast*, Allston declined to undertake any but recommended Morse. However, in February, 1837, the committee selected John Vanderlyn, Robert Weir, Henry Inman, and, most surprisingly, John Gadsby Chapman.

Morse was utterly unprepared for the rejection and, not surprisingly, unable to comprehend it. It has often been said, and Morse believed it to be true, that John Quincy Adams had engineered his catastrophe. Adams was supposed to have taken umbrage at an unsigned article in the *Evening Post* ridiculing his preference for European artists, to have wrongly believed Morse the author, and accordingly to have blocked his nomination.

It seems much more likely that Morse's obstreperous excursions into partisan politics had doomed his fondest dream. It is in character that he would fail to see himself as a figure of controversy that would make his talent irrelevant. He had inherited a polemical spirit from his father and preferred to see himself as wronged, not wrongheaded. To Allston he wrote (March 21):

To all human appearances the object of my studies for twenty-six years and the special mark at which I have aimed for fifteen years, are forever removed from before me and under circumstances particularly crying and humiliating. I need not repeat . . . the struggles and sacrifices I have made . . . to keep myself prepared for a great work of the kind long held up by the government to lure the artist of ambition to make just such exertions and sacrifices as I have made.

The Goldfish Bowl

c. 1835. Oil on wood, 29⅝ x 24⅞″
National Museum of American Art,
Smithsonian Institution, Washington, D.C.
Gift of Mrs. J. Wright Rumbough in loving
memory of her father, Gilbert Colgate

This genre-like interior is actually a portrait group: Morse's sister-in-law Mrs. Richard Cary Morse and her children, Elizabeth Ann Morse and the infant Charlotte Morse. The Greek Revival interior and its Empire furnishings are invested with a combination of sobriety and charm, a rigorous structure enveloped by a warm, glowing palette. The Madonna-like composure of Mrs. Morse may allude to the Calvinist sentiment of domestic virtue, as well as the harmony and devotion that prevailed in her household.

The Reverend Thomas Harvey Skinner

c. 1836–37. Oil on millboard, 29½ x 24½"
Museum of Fine Arts, Boston

Like most of his other late works, Morse's portrait of the Reverend Skinner (1791– 1871) was not commissioned. Seldom seen, it deserves a high place among American portraits of clergymen. Skinner taught at Andover Theological Seminary and was a founder of Union Theological Seminary. The masterful, concise composition is matched by the concentration on character. The intellectual thrust of the head is heightened by the fixed, moody gaze and the incursion of shadow onto mouth and chin. Morse's brushwork is lively throughout, as is his skillful manipulation of light.

The Muse—Susan Walker Morse

c. 1836–37. Oil on canvas, 73¾ x 57⅝"
The Metropolitan Museum of Art, New York
Bequest of Herbert L. Pratt, 1945

The New York Mirror for May 27, 1837, praised this sophisticated work in all its details, which together "constitute this picture the most perfect full-length portrait that we remember to have seen from an American artist." In pose and appearance Susan Morse (1819–1885) is similar to the foreground student in the Gallery of the Louvre, who may also be Susan.

The complexities of Morse's personality are thrown into striking perspective when we look at the portrait of his daughter, Susan Walker Morse, known as *The Muse*, painted as the ultimate crisis of his life as an artist unfolded. Exhibited at the National Academy a few weeks after the letter to Allston, it is poised, monumental, calm. It belies utterly the emotional trauma he had incurred, which threatened physical collapse. Painted in the New York University studio when Susan Morse was about seventeen, the work seems to be virtually a summary of classical design principles. She is indeed raised to the level of a muse, for she is cast in a heroic mold that recalls Baroque paintings of prophets and sibyls. The sketchbook she holds is a tabula rasa, awaiting her inspiration. Here, as always, Samuel Morse is an artist of stasis and poise, and, as in his history paintings, an intellectual artist striving for symbolic significance.

EXERTIONS AND SACRIFICES

The Muse—Susan Walker Morse

VIII. "I Never Was a Painter"

THE THUNDERBOLT OF HIS REJECTION by Congress humiliated Samuel Morse. His despair was certainly justified, and to continue in his profession as artist and promoter of the arts in America must have seemed a thankless and abhorrent prospect. His fellow artists understood his reaction well. "I have learned with mortification and disappointment that your name was not among the *chosen*," wrote Thomas Cole, "and I have feared that you would carry into effect your resolution of abandoning the art and resigning the presidency of our Academy. I sincerely hope you will have reason to cast aside that resolution. . . . You are the keystone of the arch" (March 14, 1837).

In a remarkable display of generosity and concern, a group of friends and artists raised three thousand dollars, which they presented to Morse as a "commission" to paint a historical subject of his choice. The painting was to remain his property. "The effect was electrical," wrote Thomas Cummings later. Morse was deeply moved and determined to paint "The Signing of the First Compact on board the Mayflower"—the subject he had hoped to paint for the Capitol—and to paint it the size of the Capitol paintings. This spirit of defiance was short-lived. Though he went to Massachusetts that summer to make preparatory studies, the project was never truly begun, and in 1841 he started repaying the money to his friends.

The genteel poverty in which Morse lived for years after his return from Europe wounded his pride. Writing in 1841, still in straitened circumstances, he lamented the "prospects of wealth, domestic enjoyments" that he had willingly postponed to further his art, which now seemed unattainable in that realm. The expectation of financial reward and personal renown is a theme that runs through thirty years of his correspondence, but, as Brooke Hindle reminds us, "this was not a character defect but a part of the life of the time, encouraged by the patent system and by the models and values surrounding the prevailing concept of invention."

Lack of funds also hindered the development of the telegraph, to which he now turned as he sought to block out "the blow I received from Congress." At this critical juncture, Alfred Vail, a recent graduate of New York University, offered financial and technical assistance. His father, Judge Stephen Vail, was owner of the Speedwell Iron Works in Morristown, New Jersey, where the necessary instruments for the telegraph could be fabricated. Then thirty years old, Vail accepted a fourth interest in Morse's enterprise in return for money advanced.

The partnership also led to the portraits—presumably Morse's last—of Vail's parents. Stephen Vail recorded the painter/inventor's arrival in his journal (October 28, 1837): "Professor SFB Morse of the University at N York came here last Evening to See us and take Mrs Vails & my own Likenesses." But on the following day he noted: "Morse is quite unwell this forenoon this evening took Medison—Doc Cutler attend him." The illness was fairly serious, as Morse wrote to Sidney on November 8:

You will perhaps be surprised to learn that I came out here to be sick. I caught a severe cold the day I left New York from the sudden change of temperature, and was taken down the next morning with one of my bilious attacks, which, under other treatment and circumstances, might have resulted seriously. But, through a kind Providence, I have been thrown among most attentive, and kind, and skilful friends, who have treated me more like one of their own children than like a stranger. . . . This sickness will, of course, detain me a while longer than I intended, for I must finish the portraits before I return.

It is likely that these portraits, like many of his last works, were painted gratuitously, out of friendship for the Vails and in acknowledgment of their vital support of the telegraph.

On January 24, 1838, Morse demonstrated the telegraph in his university studio for friends, and on February 8 repeated the demonstration at the Franklin Institute in Philadelphia. In Washington the Commerce Committee room in the Capitol was made available to him for the installation of his equipment. Skeptical congressmen were shown the invention, and President Martin Van Buren and his Cabinet witnessed its operation on February 21.

Morse had already filed a caveat—a preliminary request for a patent—with the U.S. Patent Office, and in May he embarked for Europe in an attempt to secure patents in England and France, the first round in a fight that lasted years in various countries. More interesting for Morse the artist was his encounter with Louis-Jacques-Mandé Daguerre.

Daguerre, like Morse, was an artist, and already the inventions that would be synonymous with their names and eclipse their art were the talk of the town. "I am told every hour," wrote Morse, "that the two great wonders of Paris just now, about which everybody is conversing, are Daguerre's wonderful results in fixing permanently the image of the *camera obscura*, and Morse's Electro-Magnetic Telegraph, and they do not hesitate to add that, beautiful as are the results of Daguerre's experiments, the invention of the Electro-Magnetic Telegraph is that which will surpass, in the greatness of the revolution to be effected, all other inventions" (March 2, 1839).

Morse's admiration for Daguerre was not lessened by his own youthful attempts to achieve the same end. On March 9 he wrote his brothers:

You have, perhaps, heard of the Daguerreotype. . . . It is one of the most beautiful discoveries of the age. I don't know if you recollect some experiments of mine in New Haven, many years ago, when I had my painting-room next to Professor Silliman's,—experiments to ascertain if it were possible to fix the image of the camera obscura. *I was able to produce different*

Bethiah Youngs Vail

1837. Oil on canvas, 30 x 25″
From the collection of Historic Speedwell, Morristown, New Jersey

The rather skeptical expression of Mrs. Vail (1778–1847) apparently disguised a warm heart. During his illness at their home, Morse wrote: "Mrs. Vail has been a perfect mother to me; our good Nancy Shepard can alone compare with her. Through her nursing and constant attention I am now able to leave my room . . . and hope to be out in a few days."

Judge Stephen Vail

1837. Oil on canvas, 30 x 25″
From the collection of Historic Speedwell, Morristown, New Jersey

Founder of the Speedwell Iron Works, which used rather than made iron, Judge Vail (1780–1864) was a shrewd entrepreneur who perceived the financial potential of the telegraph. When Alfred Vail and Morse fell behind in their schedule, he was displeased, though when the apparatus was finally ready for demonstration on January 6, 1838, he supplied the message: "A patient waiter is no loser." On January 11 the first public exhibition took place, and Morse wrote: "We have shown it to the Morristown people with great éclat . . . The success is complete." The local newspaper, The Jerseyman, *reported that "Time and distance are annihilated."*

Bethiah Youngs Vail

Judge Stephen Vail

degrees of shade on paper, dipped into a solution of nitrate of silver, by means of different degrees of light, but finding that light produced dark, and dark light, I presumed the production of a true image to be impracticable, and gave up the attempt. M. Daguerre has realized in the most exquisite manner this idea.

This letter, which included a fairly detailed description of the process, appeared in the *New-York Observer* on May 18, the first published account in America.

Two weeks later Morse sailed for home. Upon his arrival, he found that his partner and other colleagues in telegraphy had done little to advance the cause. He reproved them in a letter to the self-serving Congressman F.O.J. Smith: "My only means of support are in my profession, which I have been compelled to abandon entirely for the present, giving my undivided time and efforts to this enterprise. I return with not a farthing in my pocket, and have to borrow even for my meals. . . . If the enterprise is to be pursued, we must all in our various ways put the shoulder to the wheel."

His interest in Daguerre and his invention continued. Through Morse's nomination, the Frenchman became an honorary member of the National Academy of Design. Morse had absorbed the principles of the daguerreotype and sent a prophetic, insightful letter to Allston: "I have the instruments on the point of completion, and if it be possible I will yet bring them with me to Boston, and show you the beautiful results of the brilliant discovery." He continued:

Art is to be wonderfully enriched by this discovery. How narrow and foolish the idea which some express that it will be the ruin of art, or rather artists, for every one will be his own painter. One effect, I think, will undoubtedly be to banish the sketchy, slovenly daubs that pass for spirited and learned; those works which possess mere general effect without detail, because, forsooth, detail destroys general effect. Nature, in the results of Daguerre's process, has taken the pencil into her own hands, and she shows that the minutest detail disturbs not the general repose. Artists will learn how to paint, and amateurs, or rather connoisseurs, how to criticise, how to look at Nature, and, therefore, how to estimate the value of true art. Our studies will now be enriched with sketches from nature which we can store up during the summer, as the bee gathers her sweets for winter, and we shall thus have rich materials for composition and an exhaustless store for the imagination to feed upon.

In his own experiments with the daguerreotype, Morse was hampered by the inferior quality of the plates at his disposal. "Still I was able to verify the truth of Daguerre's revelations. The first experiment crowned with any success was a view of the Unitarian Church from the window on the staircase from the third story of the New York City University. . . . It was in September, 1839. The time, if I recollect, in which the plate was exposed to the action of light in the camera was about fifteen minutes. The instruments, chemicals, etc., were strictly in accordance with the directions in Daguerre's first book."

Morse's own daguerreotype plates have mostly disappeared or are unrecognized. A number of them were given by him to the newly founded Vassar College but are presently unlocated. Most of his experiments, as with other pioneers of the daguerreotype, were with portrait subjects, despite the fact that the long ex-

ABRAHAM BOGARDUS (1822–1908)
Samuel Finley Breese Morse

c. 1864. Photograph,
albumen silver print, 3⅝ x 2⅛"
National Portrait Gallery,
Smithsonian Institution, Washington, D.C.

By the time this photograph was taken, Morse was widely known as the father of American photography. Though similar, the camera beside him does not appear to be his first instrument, which was constructed at New York University in 1839 by George Prosch.

I NEVER WAS A PAINTER

posure time needed for the early plates resulted either in blurred images or sitters with closed eyes.

That Morse, a portrait painter in practice if not by choice, should have immediately attempted daguerreotype portraits, despite Daguerre's admonition that it was impossible, comes as no surprise. Whether he or his university colleague John W. Draper produced the first successful portrait image is uncertain. Draper claimed the honor for himself, while Morse simply recorded: "If mine were the first, other experimenters soon made better results, and if there are any who dispute that I was the first, I shall have no argument with them.... I esteem it but the natural carrying out of the wonderful discovery, and that the credit was after all due to Daguerre." A rare plate that has won expert acceptance as the work of Morse is the tiny *Portrait of a Young Man* reproduced here, judged to date from early 1840.

Although Morse seems to have stopped experimenting with the new process after two or three years, it represents a continuation of his art. As far as is known, he never painted again, yet the thought of his "profession" never entirely left him. In February, 1841, he wrote: "I have not painted a picture since that decision in Congress, and I presume that the mechanical skill I once possessed in the art has suffered by the unavoidable neglect. I may possibly recover this skill, ... if anything can tune again an instrument so long unstrung.... I am at present engaged in taking portraits by the Daguerreotype.... My ultimate aim is the application of the Daguerreotype to accumulate for my studio models for my canvas."

His day-to-day existence continued to be tenuous. A pupil of that period remembered that "he was very poor." Morse admonished him: "Don't be an artist. It means beggary. Your life depends upon people who know nothing of your art and care nothing for you. A house-dog lives better, and the very sensitiveness that stimulates an artist to work keeps him alive to suffering."

In 1841 he once again ran for mayor of New York on the Native American ticket, but fraudulent announcements that he had withdrawn his candidacy doomed it. Attempts to convince Congress to fund the telegraph continued. At the end of 1842 Morse was stringing wires for another demonstration through a vault below two committee rooms. To his astonishment he discovered the plaster cast of the 1812 *Dying Hercules* that he had given Charles Bulfinch, architect of the Capitol, twenty years earlier. Whether it had been abandoned or stored there he never knew. But it was the only survivor among six casts and is now preserved at Yale.

Congressional action on the Report on the Telegraph inched along at a snail-like pace. "I am still *waiting, waiting*.... I am exceedingly tried.... I am still kept in suspense"—these are his plaints in January, 1843. Finally, on February 21, a $30,000 appropriation bill to test further the merits of the telegraph passed the House, though an amendment requiring "that one half of the said sum shall be appropriated for trying mesmeric experiments" had first to be defeated.

Allston wrote a spirited letter of congratulations, to which the sensitive Morse replied, in part: "'What has become of painting?' I think I hear you ask.

Portrait of a Young Man

Early 1840. Ninth-plate daguerreotype,
2½ x 2⅛″ including presentation mat
Gilman Paper Company Collection, New York

Signed with a stenciled stamp on the mat, this tiny plate may be one of Morse's first attempts. It is surely one of the rare acceptable attributions known. By comparison with a much later oil portrait (with the same provenance), the sitter has been tentatively identified as the Reverend Reuben Nelson (1818–1879), a native New Yorker.

Ah, my dear sir, when I have diligently and perseveringly wooed the coquettish jade for twenty years, and she then jilts me, what can I do? . . . I shall not give her up yet in despair, but pursue her even with lightning, and so overtake her at last." Allston's death in August, 1843, brought Morse posthaste to Boston, where he adoringly examined the unfinished *Belshazzar's Feast* and took as a keepsake a brush recently used on the painting.

Morse's remark that he would pursue painting "even with lightning" indicated his desire, soon to be communicated to the government, to transfer his patent to the United States in exchange for $100,000, so that he might resume painting without fear of poverty.

The $30,000 appropriation permitted the construction of the famous telegraph line between Washington and Baltimore. On May 24, 1844, a distinguished company including members of Congress and the dowager Dolley Madison gathered in the Supreme Court chamber in the Capitol Building. The first message, now known to every American schoolchild—"What hath God wrought!"—was sent over the first intercity line in the world to Baltimore and returned in verification to Washington by Alfred Vail. Though not chosen by Morse, the famous words were certainly appropriate for him. Taken from the Bible (Numbers 23), they were part of a prophetic utterance of vindication that must have given him consolation:

> *God brought them out of Egypt;*
> > *he hath as it were the strength of a unicorn.*
> *Surely there is no enchantment against Jacob,*
> > *neither is there any divination against Israel:*
> *according to this time it shall be said of Jacob*
> > *and of Israel,*
> *What hath God wrought!*

"That sentence," wrote Morse, "was divinely indited, for it is in my thoughts day and night. 'What hath God wrought!' It is his work, and He alone could have carried me thus far through all my trials and enabled me to triumph over the obstacles, physical and moral, which opposed me."

Tape with Recorded Message

1844.
National Museum of American History,
Smithsonian Institution, Washington, D.C.

Below the symbols of the Morse Code, the Roman letters of the historic message were written as received.

Morse's offer to sell his patent to the government was refused. Unable to return to his art, he had to pursue his invention to its profitable end. He returned to Europe in August, 1845, his growing fame preceding him, to demonstrate the superiority of his telegraphic mechanism over others that had been developed and to pursue foreign patents. He traveled widely for two months. France again pleased him: "I receive a welcome here to which I was a perfect stranger in England. How deep this welcome may be I cannot say, but if one must be cheated I

CHRISTIAN SCHUSSELE (1826–1879)
Portrait study of Samuel F. B.
Morse, for Men of Progress

c. 1862. Oil on canvas
on beaverboard, c. 14¾ x 11¼″
National Museum of American History,
Smithsonian Institution, Washington, D.C.

This portrait accords with Nathaniel
Parker Willis's description of "Morse,
with his kind, open, gentle countenance,
the very picture of goodness and sincerity."

like to have it done in a civil and polite way." But Paris the art capital no longer beckoned him. "Will you believe," he wrote to Cooper four years after, "when last in Paris in 1845, I did not go into the Louvre, nor did I visit a single picture gallery."

Yet one last tantalizing opportunity to paint for the Capitol was dangled before him. Henry Inman had died without completing his commission, and Morse's supporters submitted a petition to Congress on his behalf early in 1846. In a triumph of hope over experience, Morse thought it "not improbable that [the panel] may be given me to execute," although he added: "This is but castle-building. I am quite indifferent as to the result. . . ."

It has always seemed a mystery to me how I should have been led on to the acquirement of
the knowledge I possess of painting . . . and then suddenly be stopped as if a wall were built

across my path, so that I could pursue my profession no longer. . . .

And now, if not greatly deceived, I have a glimpse of [God's] wonderful, truly wonderful, mercy towards me. He has chosen thus to order events that my mind might be concentrated upon that invention which He has permitted to be born. . . . And at the moment when all has been accomplished which is essential to its success, He so orders events as again to turn my thoughts to my almost sacrificed Isaac.

He was greatly deceived. William H. Powell of Ohio was awarded the commission in 1847 and responded in time with the undistinguished *Discovery of the Mississippi by De Soto.* Both the artist and the subject chosen proclaimed the shift in national power from the East to the West.

Morse had resigned his presidency of the National Academy two years before. Twenty-five years of active life, growing fame and, at long last, fortune lay ahead. But as a painter he was through. He began to enjoy the benefits of his growing income. In 1847 he bought the first home he had ever owned, a property he called Locust Grove on the Hudson River near Poughkeepsie, New York. For the first time in twenty years he had his three children living with him. The following year he married his twenty-five-year-old second cousin, Sarah Elizabeth Griswold, who was hearing- and speech-impaired, and who, therefore, "should add to personal affection, the feeling of gratitude for befriending her."

Morse's 1849 letter to Cooper had summarized his bitter feeling about his career as an artist:

Painting has been a smiling mistress to many, but she has been a cruel jilt to me. I did not abandon her, she abandoned me. I have taken scarcely any interest in painting for many years. . . . Except some family portraits valuable to me from their likenesses only, I could wish that every picture I ever painted was destroyed. I have no wish to be remembered as a painter, for I never was a painter; my ideal of that profession was perhaps too exalted. I may say, is too exalted.

It is clear once more that for Morse "painter" meant "history painter."

He ran unsuccessfully for Congress as a Democrat in 1854, and while he fared better than in his two races for mayor, he was less than candid about his position on the question of opening the Nebraska territory to slavery. He hedged on the issue, although in fact he believed that "slavery *per se* is not sin. It is a social condition ordained from the beginning of the world for the wisest purposes, benevolent and disciplinary, by Divine wisdom." This position was known to some, and his published anti-immigration stance was known to many. Scripture was cited by both sides in the debate over slavery. Morse also derived his pro-slavery views, though perversely, from fundamental tenets of Calvinist orthodoxy: "There is not a living thing born into this world which is . . . more perfectly enslaved as man," he wrote in his notebook. The 1854 campaign was his last.

Soon thereafter he associated himself with the young Cyrus Field in the heroic undertaking of the laying of the Atlantic cable, a feat he had predicted. In four attempts over ten years the cable snapped four times. Finally in 1866 the cable was successfully laid. In that same year, disillusioned with the United States in the post-Civil War period, hoping to give his four children by the second marriage some European education, and desirous to see the Universal Exposition in Paris, Samuel F. B. Morse and family set sail for France.

The celebrated American settled at No. 10, Avenue du Roi de Rome (now Avenue Kléber), quite near the Arc de Triomphe. The appearance of the stern Calvinist on the stage of Paris at the acme of its worldly brilliance during the reign of Napoleon III was not without irony, as we have remarked. The taste for pretense, in life and in art, was highly developed and esteemed. What must he have thought of the contemporary advertisement for "photo-painting," in which a photographic portrait was enlarged onto a canvas and painted quickly, where "an ordinary painter would require three weeks to a month's time at least!"

But Morse was a complete Francophile now and content to enjoy the honors that European nobility bestowed upon him. The Universal Exposition was "the world in epitome." "Paris now is the great centre of the world. Such an assemblage of sovereigns was never before gathered, and I and mine are in the midst of the great scenes and fêtes. We were honored, a few evenings ago, with cards to a very select fête given by the emperor and empress at the Tuileries." Such was the scene before the collapse of the Second Empire in the debacle of the Franco-Prussian War—a last burst of glory that paralleled that of Morse himself.

The complexities of the man were apparent at every turn. He was restless, ambitious, idealistic, pious, and thoroughly engaged in the great issues of the momentous century in which he lived. Samuel Morse, "made for a painter," stopped painting at the midpoint of his life because his elevated conception of the art was at odds with that of his countrymen. The citizens of the nation, still in its adolescence, did not want instruction but validation of their uniqueness. The portrait was the purest form of the democratic art, but Morse, though democrat and nativist, had ideals in art that he was determined to propagate. That he was unable to recognize his own high achievement does not prevent us from doing so.

Morse did recognize that his telegraph would "surpass, in the greatness of the revolution to be effected, all other inventions" of his time. But he was not two men. The mind that conceived of the telegraph as an instrument of instantaneous communication of information was the same mind that grasped the potential of the portrait as a means of candid communication of a person's character and life history. The telegraph bridged great distances; the portrait bridged the span of years. These two irradiant achievements were conceived and matured, in Morse's own phrase, in the studio of his brain.

Morse's Home in Paris

Morse wrote on September 22, 1866: "We are fortunate in having apartments in a new building, or rather one newly and completely repaired throughout.... [It is] within a few minutes walk of the Champ de Mars, so that we shall be most eligibly situated to visit the great Exposition when it opens in April." The building still stands (it is now No. 10, Avenue Kléber), with an inscription above the door: "J. Delisle, Arch. 1865."

Chronology

Events in Samuel F. B. Morse's Life

Political and Cultural Events

1791   *Born April 27 in Charlestown, Massachusetts*
Division over Alexander Hamilton's U.S. fiscal policies leads to establishment of Federalist and Republican parties (1792)

1793   George Washington and John Adams reelected; Louis XVI guillotined (January 21); outbreak of war between England and France, U.S. remains neutral

1794   Semaphore telegraph introduced in France

1796   Washington's Farewell Address; Adams elected president

1799   *Enters Phillips Academy, Andover, Massachusetts*
U.S. capital moved to Washington

1801   Thomas Jefferson becomes president

1803   The U.S. purchases the Louisiana Territory from Napoleon, doubling size of the country

1804   Napoleon proclaimed emperor of France

1805–10 *Attends Yale College; classes in electrical science under Benjamin Silliman and Jeremiah Day; paints watercolor miniatures*
Robert Fulton's *Clermont* steams up the Hudson from New York to Albany (1807); James Madison becomes fourth president (1809)

1810   *Washington Allston encourages Morse in his painting; works for a Charlestown bookseller*

1811   *Paints* The Landing of the Pilgrims at Plymouth; *sails for England July 13 with Allston and wife; studies with Allston and at the Royal Academy, receiving some instruction from Benjamin West; shares rooms with painter Charles Robert Leslie*

1812   *Models a plaster statuette of* The Dying Hercules, *which wins gold medal at the Society of Arts*

U.S. declares war on England (June 18)

1813   *Paints and exhibits at the Royal Academy his* Dying Hercules *to much acclaim; in the fall travels to Bristol, where he receives some portrait commissions*

Oliver Hazard Perry wins battle of Lake Erie

1814   *Returns to Bristol with Allston in the summer, but has no success among local patrons; hopes to visit Paris*
Napoleon abdicates; British troops burn Washington; war ended by Treaty of Ghent (December 24)

1815   *Morse's* Judgment of Jupiter *refused by the Academy because he is leaving England; sails for America August 21, arrives Boston October 18*
        Napoleon's return and march on Paris (March); defeated at Waterloo (June)

1816   *Exhibits his* Dying Hercules *at the Pennsylvania Academy of the Fine Arts; paints family portraits; goes to Concord, New Hampshire, in search of portrait commissions; becomes engaged to Lucretia Pickering Walker*

1817   *Paints in Portsmouth, New Hampshire; returns to Charlestown, where he paints and works on inventions*
        James Monroe becomes president

1818   *Spends winter in Charleston, South Carolina; has many sitters, including Colonel William Drayton; marries in the fall; goes to Charleston for the winter*

1819   *Commissioned to paint President Monroe for Charleston; first child born; portraits of missionaries to Hawaii*
        Treaty with Spain cedes Florida to U.S.; national financial panic

1820   *Spends winter in Charleston; portrait of Robert Young Hayne*
        The Missouri Compromise; Maine admitted as a free state

1821   *Last season in Charleston; paints in New Haven and Washington; begins* The House of Representatives
        Missouri admitted as a slave state (August 10)

1822–23 *Completes and exhibits* The House of Representatives
        The Monroe Doctrine (1823)

1824   *Accepted as member of first U.S. legation to Mexico, but the mission is postponed indefinitely; paints his wife with their two children*

1825   *Portrait of the Marquis de Lafayette commissioned; Morse's wife dies*
        John Quincy Adams becomes sixth president; completion of the Erie Canal

1826   *A founder and first president of the National Academy of Design; portrait of De Witt Clinton; delivers his "Lectures on the Affinity of Painting with the Other Fine Arts"*
        James Fenimore Cooper publishes *Last of the Mohicans*

1828   Baltimore and Ohio Railroad begun; death of Gilbert Stuart

1829   *At Cooperstown, New York, paints* View from Apple Hill; *in November sails to Europe*
        Andrew Jackson becomes seventh president

1830   *Travels in France and Italy, studying Old Masters; begins portrait of Bertel Thorvaldsen*
        July Revolution in Paris; Webster-Hayne debate in Congress on nature of the union; Polish revolution

1831   *Further travel in Italy and France; paints landscapes; begins* Gallery of the Louvre
        Uprisings in the Papal States; beginning of abolitionist movement in U.S.; Polish revolution crushed

1832   *Deep friendship with Fenimore Cooper; returns to New York in November; during voyage conceives the telegraph; appointed to faculty of New York University*
        Nullification convention in South Carolina

1833   *Completes* Gallery of the Louvre; *its exhibition is a failure*

1834   *Portrait of the Reverend William Buell Sprague*

1835   *Publication of his* Foreign Conspiracy against the Liberties of the United States

1836   *Runs for mayor of New York on Native American ticket; work on telegraph continues; portrait of his daughter, Susan Walker Morse (1836–37)*
        Samuel Colt patents the "six-shooter"

1837   *Publishes* Confessions of a French Catholic Priest; *passed over by Congress for Capitol Rotunda commission; Alfred Vail brings financial and technical assistance to telegraph project; paints last works*
John Deere introduces the steel plow; Martin Van Buren becomes eighth president; financial panic; Victoria becomes queen of England

1838   *Demonstrates telegraph to president and congressmen; sails to Europe to secure patents; meets Louis Daguerre and publishes first American description of daguerreotype*
Underground railroad organized

1839   *Experiments with daguerreotype*

1841   *Runs again for mayor of New York*

1843   *Congress appropriates funds for Baltimore-Washington telegraph line; Washington Allston dies*

1844   *First intercity telegraph message sent*

1845   *Returns to Europe to pursue patents*

1846   *Leading American artists petition Congress to award him last Capitol Rotunda commission*
War with Mexico begins

1847   *Congress does not award him the commission; buys first home, Locust Grove, on the Hudson River in New York*

1848   *Marries Sarah Elizabeth Griswold*
Revolutions in Europe

1850   Compromise of 1850

1852   Napoleon III becomes emperor of France

1854   *Runs for Congress as a Democrat*
Matthew Perry's treaty opens Japan to commerce with the U.S.

1855   *Joins Cyrus Field in venture to lay an Atlantic telegraph cable*

1861   Abraham Lincoln becomes sixteenth president

1861–65   The Civil War

1865   Assassination of Lincoln; Andrew Johnson succeeds

1866   *Cable successfully laid; sails to France with his family, where he remains until mid-1868; honorary commissioner, Universal Exposition (1867)*

1869   Ulysses S. Grant becomes eighteenth president

1870–71   Franco-Prussian War; foundation of the German empire

1871   *Statue of Morse unveiled in Central Park; farewell telegraph message sent around the world*

1872   *Dies on April 2; buried in Greenwood Cemetery, Brooklyn, with his brothers*

Bibliography

RECENT PUBLICATIONS

LARKIN, OLIVER. *Samuel F. B. Morse and American Democratic Art*. Boston, 1954.

MABEE, CARLETON. *The American Leonardo: A Life of Samuel F. B. Morse*. New York, 1943. The standard comprehensive life of Morse, except for his art.

STAITI, PAUL J. *Samuel F. B. Morse and the Search for the Grand Style*. Ann Arbor, Michigan: University Microfilms, 1979. First work by the leading Morse researcher.

EARLIER WORKS

DUNLAP, WILLIAM. *History of the Rise and Progress of the Arts of Design in the United States*. New York, 1834; new edition, revised, enlarged, and edited by Alexander Wyckoff. 3 vols. New York, 1965. Essential source by an older contemporary who also studied with West.

MORSE, EDWARD LIND, ed. *Samuel F. B. Morse: His Letters and Journals*. 2 vols. Boston, 1914. Understandably gentle to his father's faults, he still provides the easiest access to Morse's own words.

MORSE, SAMUEL F. B. *Lectures on the Affinity of Painting with the Other Fine Arts*. Edited with an Introduction by Nicolai Cikovsky, Jr. Columbia, Missouri, and London, 1983.

PRIME, SAMUEL IRENEUS. *Life of Samuel F. B. Morse*. New York, 1875. The official biography; valuable.

IMPORTANT ARTICLES

CREAN, HUGH R. In *The American Art Journal* 16 (Winter, 1984): 76–81. On the choice of Old Master paintings included in *Gallery of the Louvre*.

STAITI, PAUL J. In *Art in the Lives of South Carolinians: Nineteenth Century Chapters*, edited by David Moltke-Hansen (Charleston, 1979): PSa 1–13, PSb 1–14. On patronage and taste in Charleston when Morse worked there. In *Winterthur Portfolio* XVI (1981): 253–81. On Morse's stylistic development to about 1820.

TATHAM, DAVID. In *The American Art Journal* 13 (Autumn, 1981): 38–48. On the figures in the foreground of *Gallery of the Louvre*.

EXHIBITION CATALOGUES

Samuel F. B. Morse: American Painter. Metropolitan Museum of Art, 1932. The first retrospective exhibition of Morse's paintings, with a list of known works, whether located or not, and a biographical and critical essay by Harry B. Wehle.

Morse Exhibition of Arts and Science.... National Academy of Design, New York, 1950. In honor of Morse as a founder and first president of the Academy.

Samuel F. B. Morse ... His Affiliation with South Carolina. Columbia Museum of Art, Columbia, South Carolina, 1966.

"A Man of Genius": The Art of Washington Allston (1779–1843). Museum of Fine Arts, Boston, 1979. Important essays by William H. Gerdts (paintings) and Theodore E. Stebbins, Jr. (drawings).

Benjamin West and His American Students. National Portrait Gallery, Washington, D.C., 1980. Important text by Dorinda Evans.

Samuel F. B. Morse: Educator and Champion of the Arts in America. National Academy of Design, New York, 1982. With essays by Paul J. Staiti on Morse's ideology and politics and Nicolai Cikovsky, Jr., on his writings and lectures.

Samuel F. B. Morse. Grey Art Gallery and Study Center, New York University, 1982. The first exhibition based on the current state of research. Essays by Paul J. Staiti and Gary A. Reynolds. Special emphasis on the *Gallery of the Louvre*. Additional bibliography.

OTHER PUBLICATIONS

ALBERTS, ROBERT C. *Benjamin West: A Biography*. Boston, 1978.

CALLOW, JAMES T. *Kindred Spirits: Knickerbocker Writers and American Artists, 1807–1855*. Chapel Hill, North Carolina, 1967.

HARRIS, NEIL. *The Artist in American Society: The Formative Years, 1790–1860*. New York, 1966.

HINDLE, BROOKE. *Emulation and Invention*. New York, 1983. Stimulating discussion of the role of the spatial imaginations of Morse and Fulton in artistic and technological invention.

KENIN, RICHARD. *Return to Albion: Americans in England, 1760–1940*. New York, 1979.

KENNEDY, ROGER G. *Architecture, Men, Women and Money in America, 1600–1860*. New York, 1985. For the character of George Hyde Clark and Charleston, South Carolina.

MILLER, LILLIAN B. *Patrons and Patriotism*. Chicago and London, 1966.

Photograph Credits

The author and the publisher thank the museums, galleries, libraries, and private collectors who permitted the reproduction of works of art in their possession and supplied the necessary photographs. Other sources of photographs (listed by page number) are gratefully acknowledged below.

Alterman Studios, 54, 55; Hunter Clarkson, 65; Andrew Edgar, 38, 39; Theodore Flagg, 47; Greg Heins, 61; William Kloss, 151; Regina Monfort, 13; Horacio Mosquera, 81; Pollitzer, Strong, and Meyer, 95, 105; Kirk Prouty, 50; Joseph Szaszfai, 14, 15, 78, 79, 82, 83, 92, 97, 98, 110, 111.

Index

Page numbers in *italic* refer to illustrations.

158

DATE DUE